Next Steps

Social work students consistently struggle to apply theory to practice, or use the knowledge of textbooks and classrooms in the field. Vignettes and scenarios represented in textbooks are often simplistic, too tidy to be realistic, and with clean resolutions. *Next Steps: Decision Cases for Social Work Practice* highlights the complex, messy nature of social work practice in a way that is engaging to students, allowing them to step into the role of a practicing social worker. This book is a collection of decision cases from multiple areas of social work practice, designed to enhance the quality and depth of classroom case discussion and analysis. These realistic, compelling cases present dilemmas about which even experienced practitioners may disagree. This allows rich classroom discussion that enhances critical thinking, provides real-life application, and creates numerous opportunities to apply content and knowledge acquired throughout a social work education experience.

Lori D. Franklin, DSW, LCSW is a Clinical Associate Professor at the University of Oklahoma. She has previously co-authored a similar volume of decision cases, *Decision Cases for Advanced Social Work Practice* (Wolfer, Franklin, & Gray, 2013). Dr. Franklin, along with Dr. Gray, attended a week-long workshop with Terry Wolfer at the University of Texas and has been writing decision cases since 2008. She has a wide range of clinical practice experience in mental health as well as experience in social work licensure supervision. She teaches courses related to advanced direct practice in social work and an integrative seminar that utilizes the decision case teaching method.

Jonathan R. Kratz, MSW, LCSW is a Clinical Assistant Professor at the University of Oklahoma. He has an extensive background in juvenile justice and forensic social work as well as in mental health and school-based services with children and families. Most of his clinical work has been with Spanish speaking populations. He teaches across the direct practice curriculum including courses in mental health, group work, advanced clinical social work theories of practice, and the integrative seminar.

Karen A. Gray, PhD, LCSW, LSW-Admin is Professor Emeritus at the University of Oklahoma. She has an extensive history of decision case development and teaching, including co-authorship of *Decision Cases for Advanced Social Work Practice* (Wolfer, Franklin, & Gray, 2013). She has also authored two articles and three book chapters regarding decision cases. Dr. Gray's experience as a community organizer and macro practice focus, as well as her clinical experience, allows her to contribute a variety of cases that highlight multiple areas of practice. She teaches courses related to community organizing and development, practice with organizations and communities, and the integrative seminar with decision cases.

Next Steps
Decision Cases for Social Work Practice

Lori D. Franklin, Jonathan R. Kratz, and Karen A. Gray

Routledge
Taylor & Francis Group

NEW YORK AND LONDON

First published 2019
by Routledge
52 Vanderbilt Avenue, New York, NY 10017

and by Routledge
2 Park Square, Milton Park, Abingdon, Oxon OX14 4RN

Routledge is an imprint of the Taylor & Francis Group, an informa business

Library of Congress Cataloging-in-Publication Data
A catalog record for this title has been requested

ISBN: 978-1-138-49984-3 (hbk)
ISBN: 978-1-138-49985-0 (pbk)
ISBN: 978-1-351-01395-6 (ebk)

Typeset in Bembo
by Taylor & Francis Books

Contents

About the Authors

Lori D. Franklin, DSW, LCSW is a Clinical Associate Professor at the University of Oklahoma. Her teaching is in areas of mental health, direct practice, and clinical interventions. Her work with decision cases is a natural extension to her pre-academic career in mental health services and supervision, as well as her continued work in clinical supervision and practice. She can be contacted at lfranklin@ou.edu.

Jonathan R. Kratz, MSW, LCSW is a Clinical Assistant Professor at the University of Oklahoma. His teaching is primarily focused on direct practice with an emphasis on Motivational Interviewing and treating suicidality. Prior to joining the faculty at the University of Oklahoma, he worked with Spanish speaking clients in forensic, school, and family based service settings. Jonathan can be contacted at jkratz@ou.edu.

Karen A. Gray, PhD is Professor Emeritus at the University of Oklahoma. She is currently completing a book on the early years of Communities Organized for Public Service in San Antonio, the oldest and most successful Industrial Areas Foundation affiliate. She has conducted research in other areas of "macro" practice, including SNAP participants' use of Farmers' Markets.

Acknowledgments

The authors would like to thank Erik Zimmerman and all of the team at Taylor & Francis for the guidance through the process of creating and publishing this volume.

The University of Oklahoma and The Anne and Henry Zarrow School of Social Work have supported the writing of this volume through leadership, time, and support from graduate assistants. The authors would particularly like to thank our chapter co-authors Bethany Trueblood, Christina Miller, Kathy Shook McCallie, and Nicholas Dubriwny. The authors are grateful to fellow case method seminar instructors Mary Brandt, Steve Wells, Ann Riley, Tonia Caselman, Cynthia McPherson, Herman Curiel, and Jennifer Dell.

Several MSW students were involved in the transcription of interviews and editing of documents. We would like to thank Jeseney Whitacre, Rachel Baluh, and Andrea Crank for the time and energy put forth in these tedious tasks.

Jon and Lori thank spouses Erin Kratz and Rebekah Herrick for proofreading, editing, and ongoing support of our academic work.

We thank our students over the years of teaching the course who have taught us something new every time we teach a case. We have the privilege of contributing to the critical thinking and practice wisdom of newly launching students, and we take that privilege very seriously. We are honored to be a part of students' lives and appreciate all we learn from them.

Without a doubt, however, our most sincere thanks is extended to the case reporters who shared their stories bravely and openly. These social workers are a vital part of the education of future professionals who will benefit from their honesty and vulnerability expressed in a story of doubt. We appreciate them greatly and thank them for their contribution to the profession. We are forever impressed by the thoughtful, reflective, compassionate social workers we find in these interviews who strive to offer the highest quality social work services they can. Thank you.

Introduction

"But what *should* we do next?" "What would *you* do?" "What is the *right* answer?"

Instructors who use this book are likely to hear these pleas for guidance from anxious students. Students are likely to say these things because they, well, want there to be a solution that neatly uses the content of the course lectures to address a problem. Students are often fearful of judgment or harsh evaluation and may feel their job is to guess the magic answer that corresponds with the instructor's perception. This fear can stifle discussion, paralyze students from expressing opinions, or leave students confused and upset. Social work students are usually conscientious learners hoping to gain skills to help them do the "right" things to help others, perhaps not realizing that there is not a single "right" answer in most situations.

Social work is a rewarding profession, yet it is messy, confusing, difficult work that is often left unfinished, sprawling into new problems and rarely presenting easily recognizable solutions. Yet it is in that complex mire of human relationships, fraught with multiple problems, discomfort, contextual complications, and potential mistakes that social workers find their training is most needed. It is in those complex situations that social workers can make significant differences in the lives of vulnerable people who are living within that complexity, often suffering great pain. But rarely is there a perfect solution in our imperfect profession. We all wish there were, but if that were the case, everyone could be a social worker instead of people with good judgment, creative thinking, and flexibility.

This book of decision cases highlights this complexity in that it describes a situation where social workers, at a variety of different levels of education and practice experience, felt unsure how to proceed with a difficult situation. Sometimes the social worker feels everything has already been tried and there are no more options. Other times the social worker is so overwhelmed that it is difficult to know where to begin to intervene. But they all end with a social worker feeling unsure how to proceed, drowning in an intricate context, and wondering about the *next steps*.

The cases avoid easy solutions; while students may think a wise supervisor will have the answers, the social workers may have already consulted a supervisor who gave advice that did not solve the problem. Perhaps the supervisor felt just as unsure, or perhaps the social worker in the story *is* the supervisor who is just as perplexed as anyone else. Just seeking supervision isn't enough to solve a problem; a solution has to be proposed. While students may rush to form interdisciplinary teams, seek consultations from "experts", or quickly refer to other professionals, there is no guarantee that anyone else has a better idea of how to solve the problem than the social worker. Social workers must learn to work in teams and seek consultation when needed, but also must learn that our profession has provided us with specific knowledge and skills that may be exactly what is needed and we often *are* the experts. It is necessary for us to claim those unique qualities and provide our input to other professionals.

Each case or chapter in this volume was created by first interviewing a social worker in the field. The social workers may have a BSW working on the front lines in a wide range of generalist practice, an MSW student learning in practicum about the increased responsibilities that come with additional training, a recent MSW graduate launching into the world of practice without the safety net of their academic world, or an experienced MSW practitioner facing a new challenge in a new setting. With the variety of social work training and experience, we hope that the book is useful in a wide variety of courses. The text could be utilized in single classes using a decision case teaching model, or a text used in multiple courses through the curriculum as students progress in their educations.

Students, you may enjoy talking about these cases with field instructors or colleagues. Few things are as meaningful as a discussion of a complex matter with a range of professionals with different philosophical and educational experiences. As you read these cases for classes, or prepare to write analyses, you will most likely find that these cases feel more real than anything you have seen in other textbooks. You may find yourself engaged in them as if reading a short story and thinking about the characters when you least expect.

Undoubtedly, you will also find a case that rings true with your own experiences, unearths pain you thought was long buried, or disturbs you more than you are prepared to handle. This, yet again, models practice where a client's story takes an unexpected turn that leads us into our own internal discomfort or distress. It happens. The authors of this book also have cases they would prefer not to teach because they are painful. Yet we know that this is part of our training; that we must learn to address those complex emotions while not harming clients, and that we can seek support from other social workers and colleagues. Take full advantage of support when it is offered and be cognizant of your colleagues when discussing these cases in class. They might need your encouragement.

In addition to the variety of experiences on the social work education and experience spectrum, the cases are in diverse settings working with multiple populations. Students with experience in mental health, children and families, health care, community organizing, administration, or many other settings of social work practice should find a case that resonates with their interests. It empowers students to share their expertise with classmates and reinforces networking among peers. However, even if the student has no experience with a population or setting represented in the case, the method is designed to help students build confidence in decision making wherever they may practice. Students may not finish these cases as experts in a field, but they should be confident that they could enter a setting, understand the context, identify an area for intervention, and then make sound, ethical, helpful decisions about the *next steps*.

Analyzing Cases

The authors of this book have many years of experience teaching social work students utilizing decision cases. We have utilized decision cases in multiple courses: advanced practice with groups, advanced practice with families, generalist practice courses, community organizing, administration, bridging courses for advanced standing students, lifespan development courses, and diversity courses. We have developed simulations, role plays, and other activities to reinforce the concepts of the case and engage multiple types of learners. However, for many years we have taught a capstone course in the MSW program that exclusively utilizes decision cases. Students alternate weeks of either writing an analysis paper about the decision case or offering constructive feedback to a peer who is analyzing a case that week.

The assignment utilized to analyze the cases has varied, but essentially asks students to identify the contextual issues present in the case and identify a main problem. Students are asked not to just list issues or retell the story, but truly look behind the scenes about what may really be happening to create a "symptom" of a problem that is seen in a case. For instance, a conflicted relationship with a client may be a symptom of a lack of engagement. A poorly executed intervention may be a symptom of a lack of administrative structure. Students then attempt to identify a problem that, if solved to a degree, would positively affect the remaining dynamics of the case. Addressing engagement may improve many facets of a difficult relationship with a client. Clarifying administrative expectations might lead to better oversight on interventions.

This type of hypothesizing about what may lurk behind the curtain of presenting problems may cause students some anxiety. If you are a student, you may wonder, "Isn't that just making things up?" But of course, these ideas about "the problem behind the problem" are a result of our training. We think in systems and we notice the interaction of the environment. Social workers do not accept that the presenting problem is always the actual problem.

I often have used the example of parents who bring in their child for therapy. If the parents list examples of the child's "bad" behavior, failing grades, and eruptions of anger, they might look pleadingly at the social worker hoping for advice on how to "fix" their child. "He is out of control," they might say, or "There is just something wrong with him."

But do we simply accept that the child is "broken" and needs to be fixed? Of course not. Perhaps we discover that the parents are considering divorce, that an older sibling has been incarcerated, or the child has experienced profound abuse. Perhaps the parents are trying to hide their problems from the child, or they are talking to the child about problems as if the child were a friend of the same age as the parent. As we gather information, we hypothe-size that, "Oh, the real problem is that the family has not acknowledged that the abuse occurred, or they don't realize that the child carries around guilt for the parents' marital problems, or the family has constructed an elaborate story to hide their shame of the incarcerated sibling." That is resulting in the story of the acting out child. Your intervention will be much more complex than just meeting with the child and addressing these behaviors that are actually symptoms of a larger problem.

The next part of our assignment asks students to consider three ways the main problem could be addressed; both right now to handle the immediate situation, but also a strategy to address this problem so it does not continue to occur again and again. So with the previous example, we may need to address some behavior right away before this little one hurts someone or is suspended from school. But after that immediate crisis is resolved we get to the bigger task of addressing the underlying issue. If we don't, a new behavior will crop up tomorrow and we will be back at square one. So we work with the family, any number of ways, but we address the underlying concerns that are the true problem.

We ask for strategies that don't just simply say "address behaviors" or "work with the family" however. We want the gritty details that show us that social worker has a real plan of action. How exactly will you address those beha-viors? If that family is resistant, how will you even convince them to partici-pate in family therapy? Is there a particular intervention you have in mind? Are there other players in the case that need to be incorporated? What will be first and then second?

Asking for three strategies, we have found, challenges students to think further than what immediately comes to mind, and they are asked to search through evidence-based practice literature for input into crafting a plan that is specific to the case. They then choose a strategy, research it more thoroughly, and create an evaluation plan. The three strategies, all of which must be ethical and supported by evidence, emphasize that there are many ways to approach difficult situations. While one might seem better to a particular social worker, there may not be a clear right answer regarding how to pro-ceed. Often we are stuck with the age-old conundrum of "how much is enough?" And that is social work.

After the assignment is turned in, we use Socratic questioning to help stu-dents expand what they know about the case and search for an even broader understanding of the situation with their classmates. They learn from each other, sharing their very different ideas about the problems and solutions, their unique perspectives from life and practice experience, finding their own interpretations and lenses that influenced their perception of the case.

The years of teaching this course with decision-based cases has taught us that while it is difficult for students to let go of wanting answers and clear solutions, it is a new and valuable skill to sit with profound discomfort. We often do not know how our interventions are received when we lose contact or our role with a client ends. Often the part where things "get better" is far away and our piece is just one degree of realignment towards the eventual finish line. After a series of classes with examples in shaded boxes that illustrate ideal practice, this is a skill that may come as a surprise.

Karen Gray and Lori Franklin worked on a previous volume of case studies entitled *Decision Cases in Advanced Social Work Practice* (Wolfer, Franklin, & Gray, 2013). That volume also includes a wide variety of decision cases including areas of practice such as geriatric mental health, adoptions, interpersonal violence, hospice, supervision of students, veteran services, and child protection.

As Jonathan Kratz joined the decision case teaching team, he began writing new cases along with Lori Franklin and Karen Gray. We soon found that we were ready to create a collection of newer cases with additional areas of interest for students and instructors. This book is different in that it has cases from BSW practitioners as opposed to all master's cases, as well as several cases where the social worker practices macro social work in a community or organization. The book is organized progressively from the BSW practitioner to the MSW student, new MSW practitioner, then experienced MSW. But do not assume this implies the cases begin with simple dilemmas and gain complexity through the volume. We have long ago released any ideas that we know which cases are most difficult for which students, as the expertise and experience students bring to the table determine their view of difficulty. Furthermore, students often feel cases get more and more complex as the class proceeds, but we counter that perhaps they are just becoming better observers who are now more likely to see the complexity instead of oversimplifying situations. Sometimes things get harder the more you know.

For Students

So if you are a student, welcome to an experience of wonder and doubt, which we hope makes you a strong decision maker and an increasingly confident practitioner. The format of these cases may be new to you. So read them at least a week early so you have time to think about them while you eat breakfast or brush your teeth. Read the case again each day. We guarantee that you will see something new and find something else to wonder about each time. Make a list of these wonderings: the things that stand out to you or cause concern, questions that emerge, or observations of unusual circumstances. You may find the list falls into categories about the therapeutic relationship, the agency structure, the influence of policy, or many other possibilities. You will see what rises to the top as a pivotal problem, but only if you allow yourself time to look deliberately and carefully consider the nuances of the story.

We want to model for you that while there is a tendency to rush to solve problems, this often results in surface level solutions without long term efficacy. We often jump into "doing" with our theories and evidence and interventions before we truly understand the issues and barriers the client faces. So instead, take time observing and understanding the context. You are "listening" to this case story and your social worker protagonist wants you to understand the context. If you started a new job, you would hopefully take time to look and learn about the surroundings before laying out your plans to change everything and start over. So, hold yourself back from immediate, knee jerk solutions that we all have pop into our minds.

Once you have a handle on the pivotal concern and how it fits into the big picture, you are ready to think about next steps. But what have you learned about crafting interventions? What have you learned to do when you truly have no idea what to do next? You would never just try something and hope it was a good idea, but instead you would look at the literature! So now you dive in, asking the question of what a social worker would do to help with this identified problem. You will soon have at least three ideas of sound, evidence supported interventions. They may all have a different twist, but they are all a thorough plan that is ethical, effective, and tailored to the situation.

The trick is to translate the literature to the situation at hand. If I know I want to provide a cognitive behavioral intervention to a client, I may know that abstractly, but what am I really going to say? What have I gleaned from the story that indicates a starting place for this intervention, and how will I start it? And are there things I need to do first, like get to a safer place, return a phone call, or ask my client if this is even what he or she wants? These cases will challenge you to put your evidence-based practice knowledge into a real setting with real people, considering each step along the way.

For Instructors

If you are an instructor, please contact the publishers of this book so that you can access the teaching materials that are available from the authors. We provide discussion questions, assignment ideas, reflection questions, and ideas for classroom activities. They are truly a golden resource you do not want to miss.

Remember your job is to encourage thinking, not provide answers. This sounds easy but is harder than any teaching imaginable. Your Socratic questions will push students to wrestle with these cases and hopefully let go of the idea that there is one right answer they are guessing at, hoping to please you. Students are encouraged to express opinions, support them in conversation with their peers, and consider multiple aspects of issues. They gain the ability to look at many solutions to a problem, adding a sense of efficacy at problem solving without a feeling of helplessness, but also learning to analyze the pros and cons of various paths of intervention. It is a gift to see a description of three excellent, ethical, helpful, detailed interventions with a discussion of why this social worker decided one was a better choice than the others based on client fit, practitioner skill, and empirical evidence.

Students also gain the experience of putting themselves in the shoes of another social worker, who is feeling overwhelmed, unsure, and maybe a little afraid. We all wrestle with the shame of not knowing, doubts at our capabilities, our imposter worries, and our fears of doing something wrong with dire consequences. But in these cases, students can step into that feeling with the characters. There is a tendency to judge the social workers in the cases with a series of "she should have" or "he failed to" type statements. But instructors want the students to feel the situations more tangibly than that. We interviewed social workers who were good people, good practitioners, and were trying their best to do good work. So while students may see mistakes, we must keep them from separating into a stance of "I would never do that, so this does not apply to me." None of us knows what will happen in difficult situations, and even experienced "experts" have doubts. We hope to train social workers who support each other, forgive each other and themselves, and model compassion for themselves, their colleagues, and their clients.

So please enjoy the book and let us know your feedback. We look forward to hearing how you used the material and what results you found in your classroom.

Part I

Bachelor of Social Work Graduates

1 Bonnie's Boys

Bonnie Tsosie had to admit that the powwow outing had gone better than she could have ever imagined. Dozens of men in bright grass-dance regalia quickly paced around the field in perfect sync to the thunderous pulse of tribal drums that would make any rock concert seem derivative. The sunset cast a golden glow across the field, creating long shadows that amplified the dramatic expression of the dancers.

"Can we please stay a little longer?" Bruce pleaded, dropping to his knees dramatically, "It's not over yet! I want to stay until the end!"

"I'm sorry, but we really need to get back to our unit by 8 PM and I think the rest of the group is ready to go," Bonnie responded, "and you really need to get back so you can take your nighttime meds and get to bed."

"This is boring," one of the other boys interjected.

"Shut up! Don't you ruin this!" Bruce took several steps towards the boy, fists clenched. *Here we go*, Bonnie thought as she stepped between Bruce and the rest of the group from Children's Hope Residential Treatment (CHRT). *Maybe this was a bad idea after all. Bruce is like a walking time-bomb. I never know what will set him off.*

Bonnie Tsosie

Bonnie had regularly attended powwows since she was a young girl. "I'm half Indian, half hillbilly!" she would joke to anyone who asked about her heritage. Although powwows played a central role in her cultural development, they had a side benefit of giving her a reprieve from problems at home. She had been exposed to years of domestic violence as a child, first with her biological father and later with a step-father. Bonnie frequently ran away to her grandmother's home in the Winnebago Reservation to escape the abuse, but her mother would eventually come and bring her back to Omaha.

At the age of 15, Bonnie began to keep a gun under her pillow to keep her stepdad away from her at night. Her grades dropped in school, she joined a gang, and she was often expelled for fighting other students. After being held back to repeat her sophomore year, it seemed likely that Bonnie would drop out of high school.

"Junior ROTC saved my life," Bonnie would often say. She joined at the urging of a school counselor in her junior year. The JROTC sergeant took an interest in making sure that Bonnie stayed on track.

"Get your ass up! You're too smart to miss school!" he would yell as he banged on her front door when she overslept. Bonnie found comfort in the structure and consistency of JROTC and she soon began to seek out other programs like it by joining Color Guard and the rifle team, and dreaming of joining the Marines.

It took Bonnie an extra year to finish high school and nearly three years to earn her Associates degree at Metropolitan Community College (MCC) in Omaha. By the time she earned her Associates degree, Bonnie had two children and mostly put her dreams of joining the Marines on hold.

"You need to get your Bachelor of Science in Social Work (BSSW) from the University of Nebraska at Omaha," her advisor at MCC insisted. At the time Bonnie had been working at a crisis center for youth and had realized that she really enjoyed working with teenagers. As her advisor described the opportunities a BSSW would afford her in that field, she decided to go for it and became one of the first people from her family to earn a college degree.

Starting Work at Children's Hope Residential Treatment (CHRT)

Bonnie was hired as a Mental Health Technician (MHT) at CHRT within weeks of graduating with her BSSW. As an MHT, she enjoyed leading rehab groups and working on life skills with the residents. Bonnie felt a special connection to many of her clients as she would learn of their traumatic childhoods. *I know they can escape the cycle, because I'm living proof that it's possible!* By far, MHTs spent more time with the residents than any of the other professionals at CHRT.

Although Bonnie felt a strong sense of empathy for her clients, she was disciplined in maintaining strict boundaries. Orientation for new staff at CHRT featured hilariously outdated training videos from the 70s on the importance of professional boundaries in residential treatment facilities. Although the training videos provided fodder for inside jokes among CHRT staff, Bonnie was increasingly aware of the importance of clear boundaries with her clients the longer she worked at CHRT. She had witnessed the subtle way in which small boundary issues grew into major controversies within the agency. In fact, Bonnie guessed that boundary violations represented a very large percentage of employee terminations at CHRT.

Boundaries were especially problematic when CHRT hired MHTs who were only a few years older than many of the residents in the program. One afternoon Bonnie noticed a resident tapping Cristal, a newly hired MHT, on her foot under a table. She immediately pulled Cristal aside and confronted her, "What's going on out here?"

"Oh nothin', just colorin' pages with the residents," Cristal replied.

"Did you not feel him tappin' your foot?" Bonnie asked as her gaze intensified.

"Um, yeah, well I told him to quit," Cristal replied nervously.

"Right, well nobody else knows you told him to quit. You need to start removing yourself from that situation. That type of boundary violation won't do you any favors in this agency."

Bonnie's natural leadership skills cemented her reputation as an invaluable member of the CHRT staff. In fact, the administrative staff often treated Bonnie more like a supervisor than an MHT, even to the point that she was often included in weekly administrative staff meetings. Bonnie was never afraid to speak her mind, and this was a source of both strength and tension in the administrative group. She was often confronted for being "too abrasive and sassy."

Clinical Director Dennis Kodak would verbally interpret her statements in his typical Mr. Rogers fashion, saying, "What I think Bonnie is trying to say is…." *You don't have to be my buffer, I can take care of myself,* Bonnie would think whenever Dennis tried to diplomatically reframe a confrontational statement. Yet Bonnie rarely confronted him on this tendency. *He's such a sweet man and, honestly, he's just trying to keep the peace.*

"Don't you talk to me like that!"

CEO Alexander Ludwig was someone that Bonnie attempted to spend as little time with as possible. Although Alexander's role in the system was largely related to finances, he had started as an MHT decades earlier and often made a habit of walking through the units and critiquing staff.

"You need to get your shit together!" Alexander told Bonnie in front of several residents one afternoon. Bonnie had been struggling with some personal matters and was visibly upset when Alexander had walked through the room and confronted her.

"Don't you talk to me like that in front of these kids!" Bonnie yelled at Alexander in the hallway outside the unit.

"Who do you think you are to tell me what to do?" Alexander responded, "This is my hospital!"

Later that day in Dennis's office, Bonnie unloaded her frustrations. "He's always harder on me. I'm not going to let him talk to me like that, especially in front of the residents."

Dennis sat calmly behind his desk and listened attentively to Bonnie, then suggested, "You know, I think you might remind Alexander of his sister…", Dennis stopped mid-sentence in response to the extreme irritation on Bonnie's face. *Of course, he's going to psychoanalyze the CEO instead of doing something about this hostile work environment.*

"You know, I think Alexander is trying to say that he cares about you and that he wants you to succeed," Dennis continued.

"This is bullshit," Bonnie couldn't contain her irritation, "Alexander is an ass."

"I'm an ass?" Alexander interjected, surprising Bonnie who had not noticed him in the doorway behind her, "why don't you say that to my face?"

"You're an ass!" Bonnie exclaimed as she stood mere inches from Alexander, her five-foot, four-inch frame only an inch taller than his.

Bonnie fully expected to be terminated from the agency, yet her name continued to be listed on the hospital schedule. *Maybe Dennis talked Alexander into giving me a second chance?* Bonnie thought as she arrived on the unit later that same week. *Shouldn't we at least have a meeting to debrief about the argument? Are they really going to just ignore that I called the CEO an ass to his face?* Several days passed and neither Dennis nor Alexander seemed interested in discussing the incident with Bonnie.

A Special Resident

Alexander barely spoke to Bonnie in the months that followed. In fact, Alexander had become significantly less visible throughout the facility. He rarely walked through the residential units and minimally participated in weekly administrative meetings. Given this new normal in the agency, Bonnie was surprised when Alexander spoke during a meeting in early March 2015.

"We have a new resident who is transferring to us from the acute unit at CHI Immanuel," Alexander shared, appearing to direct his statement at Bonnie. "He's a 13-year-old Omaha male and he's being discharged after a suicide attempt. He's been in custody for over seven years and has been diagnosed with Reactive Attachment Disorder and Major Depression. His Department of Health and Human Services (DHHS) and Indian Child Welfare Act (ICWA) workers are at a loss about where to place him. He's gone AWOL from nearly every residential facility in the state."

Here we go again, Bonnie thought, *he's going to ask me to take the lead because I'm Native American.*

Bonnie's instinct was immediately validated as Alexander continued, "I really want Bonnie to work with this kid and develop a relationship with him." Alexander looked directly at Bonnie, "I think you will have a lot in common." Although Bonnie was annoyed by previous suggestions that she lead a Native American rehab group, she wondered if this was Alexander's way of apologizing for his role in their argument months prior.

Bruce

This kid is going to knock someone out, Bonnie thought as Bruce, a stout 13-year-old boy, walked onto the unit for the first time. Bonnie noticed him scanning the room and sizing up the other residents. *So sad to see the jailhouse mentality in such young kids,* Bonnie thought as Bruce approached her.

"Hi there, let's get you settled in," Bonnie introduced herself. Most residents would bring a small bag of permitted personal items when admitted to CHRT, but Bruce had nothing but the clothing he was wearing and a few books.

"This is Marcus," Bonnie introduced Bruce to the male MHT on duty, "he will help you get settled into your room."

Marcus was one of the most experienced MHTs at CHRT. An African American man in his late 40s, his calm yet firm style seemed to put residents at ease. In fact, Bonnie had noticed that there were significantly fewer behavioral problems on the unit when Marcus was on duty.

"What's up little man?" Marcus shook Bruce's hand, adding, "nice to have another Native brotha' to hang with Ms. B on this unit."

Bruce looked at Bonnie with a confused look on his face, "Native?"

"Don't listen to him, it's nothing," Bonnie responded.

"No, I'm serious," Marcus interrupted, "Ms. B here is Indian too."

Bonnie felt uncomfortable as Bruce looked her up and down and said, "No way. You a white girl."

"Don't let these blond highlights fool you," Bonnie said playfully. "It's okay if you don't believe me—I get that all the time."

"I'm Omaha. What tribe are you? Winnebago?" Bruce guessed correctly.

"Oh yeah, everybody's Winnebago around here, right?" Bonnie responded sarcastically. *Maybe this won't be so bad,* she thought as Marcus walked Bruce to his room. *I hate to admit it, but Alexander might have been right about me working with this kid.*

Settling In

Bonnie had always made a point of treating all of the residents at CHRT as equally as possible, yet it was clear that Bruce preferred her to the other staff. Bonnie wasn't the only one who noticed Bruce's affinity for her. Within a few weeks most of the staff had begun to call Bruce "Ms. B's Boy." Bonnie was irritated by this and often confronted staff members about the inappropriateness of the nickname.

As Bruce entered his fourth week at CHRT, Bonnie had begun to really connect with him on a cultural level. *I can't tell if he's really interested in tribal stuff or if he's pretending because he knows that it interests me,* Bonnie wondered. *What 13-year-old boy likes traditional beadwork?* Her doubts about the authenticity of his stated interest rapidly faded as he spent hours devouring books on traditional beadwork that Bonnie brought to CHRT.

"You can't do beadwork while you're here, but maybe it's something you can look into after you leave," Bonnie had told Bruce when she first gave him the books. "Please be careful with them—they technically belong to my grandmother," she warned.

"Well, when I get out I'm going to make you this one," Bruce said pointing at a photo of a particularly elaborate beaded headband.

"You know that I can't take gifts from you," Bonnie reminded Bruce. "You should make it for yourself, or maybe you could make some money by selling it."

Mom

"This is how my mom should've been," Bruce said out of the blue one afternoon as he played UNO with Bonnie in the dayroom. Bonnie didn't respond right away. *I feel so bad for him. Despite everything he's been through, he's just an innocent kid who was dealt a bad hand.* Bonnie's thoughts drifted to her own childhood. *Maybe Bruce can overcome these obstacles and find happiness like I did. I wonder if he's ever experienced a relationship as stable as the one we've developed?* Bonnie thought before finally replying to Bruce's statement, "Yeah, I'm sorry she hasn't been able to be there for you."

Bruce's behavior when Bonnie was on the unit was dramatically different compared to when she wasn't. "Reflection" was the lowest behavioral level given to clients in the program, and Bruce had just levelled up after spending time on Reflection due to a fight earlier in the week. He had yet to make it a full week at CHRT without being placed on Reflection. Bonnie was often saddened when she arrived at work to find that Bruce had dropped a level. *It's so demeaning how they prohibit him from socializing with other residents for 24 hours.* Bonnie had heard rumors of several occasions in which Bruce had been placed on Reflection for fighting with residents who said disrespectful things about her. *I think that my relationship with him is meaningful, but sometimes I wonder if I'm actually making things worse. I certainly don't need a 13-year-old running around defending my honor!*

"Time for group!" Marcus announced, interrupting the UNO game. Bonnie took a deep breath as she helped the residents arrange the dayroom chairs into a circle. Groups had been tense all week after Eric, a 17-year-old CHRT "frequent flyer," had been readmitted to the program.

"Today we are going to talk about future goals and the kinds of things we might like to do as adults," Marcus began as Eric and several other boys snickered at the unintentional innuendo.

"Eric, you seem to have something to say," Marcus continued, attempting to refocus the group. "Would you mind sharing a future goal with the group?"

"I'm going to be a UFC fighter," Eric announced as he cracked his knuckles.

"I see," Bonnie replied, "but do you understand that UFC athletes fight for sport? In our last group you shared about how your fighting is connected to your anger and I wonder if you can see the difference?"

"I see how this is," Eric answered angrily, "you're just hatin' on me. I know you don't like me, so why don't you just shut up."

"Don't tell her to shut up!" Bruce yelled at Eric.

"Don't you talk to me like that!" Eric countered as both boys stood and took a few steps towards each other.

Bonnie jumped to her feet and yelled, "Listen! This ain't worth losing your levels over! Remember that we have an outing later this week and you can't go if you're on Reflection!"

It's too late, Bonnie thought as she noticed Bruce's rapid breathing and clenched fists. *He almost never bounces back from something like this without being restrained by staff.* The boys continued to posture as Marcus and Bonnie attempted to regain control of the group, talking over each other.

"Well, come on then, bring it!" Eric threatened as he took several steps towards Bruce. Seconds later, Eric was on the ground, having been punched multiple times in the face by Bruce. Bonnie grabbed Bruce and held him as tight as she could to keep him from jumping on Eric, who appeared to have been knocked unconscious. CHRT's policy against chemical restraints meant that Bruce would need to be physically restrained until he was able to calm down. As Marcus attended to Eric, several other staff members arrived on the unit to help.

Fresh Start

"Maybe your boy just needs something to look forward to," Dennis suggested as Bonnie debriefed with him and Alexander later that day, "he knows that his DHHS and ICWA workers are probably going to place him yet another foster home after he's discharged from here, so what motivation does he have to work this treatment program?"

"Don't you go to powwows every weekend?" Alexander asked Bonnie, "Bruce sure seems to have connected to you culturally—maybe a powwow outing would incentivize him."

"I'm not so sure Bruce is ready for an outing," Bonnie countered, "I mean, he's barely functioning in here!"

"You're right, but he also can't stay in here forever," Dennis added, "with the exception of today's incident, he's a different kid when you're around. We've been trying to work with him for almost half a year, maybe something like a special outing could give him a fresh start."

"Well, there's a Christmas powwow coming up, but I'm still not so sure about this," Bonnie cautioned.

The Powwow

Dennis was right about the motivating impact of an outing to a powwow. In the three weeks leading up to the planned event, Bruce had only been placed on Reflection a single time.

"Native pride! Native pride!" Bruce chanted as he and four other residents joined Bonnie for a special pre-outing group. The other boys were significantly less enthusiastic, but seemed happy at the opportunity to leave the building for a few hours.

"Here's the deal," Bonnie began, "we can stay at the powwow for a few hours if everyone follows some basic rules."

"Yeah, if anyone disrespects us, we'll take care of them," Bruce interrupted as he wrapped his arms around the boys on either side of him.

"Well, I'm glad you bring that up, Bruce, because the first rule is that we are going to stay together the entire time and we're not going to talk to strangers. There are going to be people in traditional regalia and it is very important that you not touch anything. There will be vendors around the facility that sell a variety of traditional art and you need to know that we are not buying anything this evening. If you want to look at the art, we can all go together."

I sure hope this goes well, Bonnie thought as Cristal drove the agency van around the parking lot looking for a space to park. Bruce was practically skipping as the group walked towards the venue. The Christmas powwow was very popular and well-attended, so Bonnie was relieved when she was able to find a comfortable place for the group to sit and enjoy the festivities.

As the evening progressed, Bonnie had to admit that the powwow outing had gone better than she could have ever imagined. Dozens of men in bright grass-dance regalia quickly paced around the field in perfect sync to the thunderous pulse of the tribal drums that would make any rock concert seem derivative. The sunset cast a golden glow across the field, creating long shadows that amplified the dramatic expression of the dancers.

"Can we please stay a little longer?" Bruce pleaded, dropping to his knees in his typical dramatic fashion, "It's not over yet! I want to stay until the end!"

"I'm sorry, but we really need to get back to our unit by 8 PM and I think the rest of the group is ready to go," Bonnie responded, "You need to take your nighttime meds and get to bed soon."

"This is boring," one of the other boys interjected.

"Shut up! Don't you ruin this!" Bruce responded as he clenched his fists and took several steps towards the boy. *Here we go*, Bonnie thought as she stepped between Bruce and the rest of the group, *maybe this was a bad idea after all. Bruce is like a walking time-bomb. I never know what will set him off.*

"How about we stay for five more minutes and then we can leave?" Bonnie offered as a compromise.

"This sucks," Bruce answered as he regained his composure and began dancing again. *That was a close call*, Bonnie thought as she imagined the dozens of times Bruce had been restrained for fighting since his admission to CHRT.

As the group began making their way out of the crowded venue, Bruce made a point of delaying their departure as much as possible by stopping at every arts and crafts tent they encountered.

"I really want this! Can you please buy it for me, Momma?" Bruce asked enthusiastically gesturing at a beautiful prayer fan.

"You know that I can't buy things for you and you wouldn't be allowed to have it on the unit even if I did," Bonnie responded for what felt like the hundredth time that evening. "And please don't call me Momma, okay?"

As Bonnie was speaking she noticed her aunt and uncle strolling through the crowd. *Oh no!*, Bonnie thought as her relatives noticed her and started walking towards the group, *how do I explain to them who these kids are without violating confidentiality?*

"How wonderful to see you!" Bonnie's uncle exclaimed as he gave her a hug.

Before Bonnie could respond, Bruce declared, "Hello! I'm Bonnie's new son!"

"Is that right? Well I guess that would make you my grandnephew! Welcome to the family, son." Bonnie's uncle responded in jest.

This is wrong, Bonnie thought as she tried once again to corral the small group of boys back to the agency van. *We've gone beyond boundary problems and HIPPA violations. I can't be Bruce's family. What's going to happen when he's discharged and our relationship ends? What's the point of him connecting to me and this culture if we're just going to re-traumatize him when his time at CHRT is done? What is the right thing to do for this child?*

2 Hunger

"This is insane, I am not going to let a foster family undergoing allegations of sexual abuse convince me that Ms. Lee is doing anything wrong. This is a trusted foster parent, and there is no indication of a problem!" Permanency Services Worker Roxie Venton stated emphatically. "Just because Deja calls them mom and dad, that doesn't mean that's the best thing for her. We all know that you can remove children and they grow up and still want to go back there, even if they were beaten."

"But the court has ordered visitation with the Greens. Her attorney wants that too, and I feel like I have a duty to see if we can get Deja back in their home," responded Jake Maxwell, the Supervisor of Permanency Services.

"What?" Roxie said incredulously. "I will never agree with that. They are just obsessed with trying to make Ms. Lee look bad and get Deja back. I don't believe anything they say. I will not put an abused child back in the foster home where the abuse occurred." *I know Ms. Lee has such a sweet spirit and is so affectionate with those kids*, thought Roxie. *They all seem to love her. Surely she isn't withholding food from Deja like the Greens say. That is ridiculous. And it has to be better than the Greens.*

Child Protective Services of Kansas City

Like many states, the state of Kansas was desperately in need of foster parents to care for the children in state custody. With more than 7000 children in need of foster care, removed from homes due to abuse, neglect, drug exposure, and more, the state had fewer than 3000 licensed homes for foster care placement. While the social workers had a mission to work in partnership with families, communities, the courts, and other governmental entities to ensure safety, permanency, and well-being of children, it was often difficult to find a place to house children in need.

Roxie Venton, BSW

Roxie Venton came to social work after a career as an insurance agent. She became a Child Advocacy Special Advocate (CASA) volunteer with the court systems and enjoyed the opportunities to help children. She went to a local community college and crossed paths with a professor who introduced her to the career of social work. She transferred to the University of Missouri and by

2015 had a BSW. As a non-traditional student, Roxie perceived herself as outspoken and confident, and very motivated.

Finding work with Child Protective Services as a Permanency Worker gave her a feeling like she could relax and breathe for the first time. She had never felt comfortable in the insurance company environment, with an array of tattoos on her arms and shoulders covered and hiding the piercings in her nose and eyebrow. She now could wear short sleeves, put in her jewelry, and added colorful streaks in her black hair, bright clothing, and her bracelet engraved with "Wake up. Kick Ass. Repeat."

Roxie often was a surprise to families with a different mental picture of a social worker. But families described her as friendly and engaging, relatable, and they often appreciated her direct and honest feedback. She often would explain her love of her job by saying, *I am very confident in my ability to do this job because I really do believe that God gives everyone talent, and this is mine. It just took me a lot longer to figure it out.*

Deja's Journey

Deja Davis was removed from her biological parents after confirmations of neglect. Her older half-brother, DeAndre, had been removed several years earlier and taken to Lakeview Children's Home for long term care. DeAndre had been born with hydrocephalus and many other medical issues. At one point during his first year, his tracheotomy was obstructed, and he went without oxygen for almost 30 minutes. Since then, the child had been sustained with life support systems and his aunt provided kinship foster care.

While not on Roxie's caseload, when she became involved with Deja's case, she often visited the aunt and DeAndre at the Children's Home. While a sad situation, Roxie hoped she could eventually help the aunt secure adoption so that she could make decisions about the long term use of life support systems.

Deja was small for a 3-year-old, and very sweet and friendly. She seemed like a happy child who was obedient and quiet. She was black, dark-skinned, and wore her hair in multiple braids.

To the Greens

Although it was always preferred to place black children with black families, Deja was placed in the home of Darren Whitson, who was white, but was the foster parent of another of Deja's siblings from another previous removal. But Mr. Whitson received some threats from Deja's biological father, and Deja was moved to live with his sister and brother-in-law. The Greens were a middle-class white family with three biological children in the home aged 17, 12, and 2. Mr. Green worked with the fire department, and Mrs. Green was a caretaker for adults with developmental disabilities.

However, after about six months in the home, the Greens disclosed having discovered an incident involving their 12-year-old son. Their son confessed that he had been masturbating in the bathroom when 3-year-old Deja walked in unexpectedly. He had then forced his penis into her mouth. Deja was interviewed and indicated that the older brother had also touched her with his penis, and that Mrs. Green had slapped her. But in court, there were comments about unreliable testimony from 3-year-olds and the potential for counselors misleading young children. Despite Roxie's objections, even Deja's attorney and her CASA worker agreed it was best for Deja to go back to the Greens. The court ordered supervised visitation with the Greens, claiming she related to them as mom and dad and that bond needed to be preserved.

Grandma Lee

Roxie was pleased to find that Maxine Lee was willing to take Deja in after the removal. Ms. Lee was well known at the agency after having adopted a sibling group of four children several years earlier. She was an older black woman with a thick Southern accent. The children called her "Grandma," climbed up on her lap, and hugged and kissed her affectionately. "I hope it is ok that we go to church on Wednesdays and Sundays. And this little one will join the choir with the others," she had told Roxie at their first meeting.

Adjusting to Grandma's House

Roxie could see Deja playing outside as she pulled into the cul de sac. Deja was jumping up and down with excitement and ran to Roxie as she opened the car door. Her hair was adorable, in braids with heavy colored beads that bounced as she jumped. Roxie accepted Deja's hug, greeted Ms. Lee, and sat down on the couch.

"Oh!" Roxie exclaimed to Deja. "Looks like you have a bruise!" She pointed to the bruise she had just spotted along Deja's hairline.

"She took a little spill over there," Ms. Lee said with a little laugh. "Running so fast! She tripped over herself and bumped her head there on the end table." She pointed to a small wooden table in the entryway.

Deja giggled and leaned against Ms. Lee.

"Then she loves those big beads so much for her braids," Ms. Lee continued. "'Use those sparkly, big ones!' she'll say. And I will do it if it keeps her still when I'm braiding!"

Deja shook her head side to side to show how the beads could swing back and forth.

"But I wonder if sleeping on those big old things sometimes presses into her little head some!" Ms. Lee continued. "Probably bruises all over that head from sleeping on those things!" She picked Deja up and set her on her lap affectionately.

Got Snacks?

Roxie helped Deja buckle in to her booster seat and waved to the day care teacher.

"Alright Deja, let's go!" she said brightly. "Off to the office to see Mr. and Mrs. Green for visitation."

"Ms. Roxie, you have snacks?" Deja asked.

"Sweetie, didn't you have a snack at day care?" Roxie asked.

"Hungry," said the girl.

Roxie had a big bag of pretzels she had planned to keep in her desk drawer when she returned to the office, but she opened it and passed it back to Deja. As she glanced in the rearview mirror, she saw that Deja was pushing them into her mouth with both fists.

"Slow down there!" she exclaimed. "Don't choke yourself."

They pulled into the parking lot and Roxie unbuckled Deja from the car seat. The bag of pretzels was empty and tossed on the floor. *Oh well,* she thought. They walked to the visitation room, where Mr. and Mrs. Green were already waiting and greeted Deja. Mr. Green began reading her a book and Mrs. Green approached Roxie.

"Hello," said Mrs. Green coolly to Roxie. She was holding a bathroom scale in her hands. "Did you hear what happened during our last visit?" Roxie remembered her supervisor had overseen the previous visit.

"She just *gorged* herself!" Mrs. Green said emphatically before Roxie could respond. "We took her out to dinner and she ate a burger and fries in less than five minutes. Then she wanted ice cream and then said she was still hungry!"

"Right," Roxie said. "She does seem to eat kind of frantically."

"She ate until she threw up! We went to the park after dinner and she threw up after getting off the swing!" Mrs. Green said in a forced whisper. "That woman is starving her. Look how much weight she has lost."

"She is a tiny girl," Roxie stated.

"No!" Mrs. Green interrupted raising a finger to point at Roxie. "She is losing weight. I will show you."

She put the scale on the ground and called Deja over to stand on it. *This is completely inappropriate*, Roxie thought. *They have brought this up again and again.*

"Look at this!" Mrs. Green exclaimed. "When she lived with us she weighed 32 pounds. Now it is like 29!"

"OK, Mrs. Green," Roxie said. "It is concerning that she is developing this kind of eating pattern, but I can't help but think this is some kind of reaction to all she has been through. Kids who have been food insecure develop all kinds of behaviors surrounding food. And of course, we need to address them, but it doesn't mean she is starving. But I will check into it further."

Calling the Counselor

Roxie called Deja's counselor, hoping for some insight into the eating concerns. Emma Rink had worked with Deja during all of her foster placements.

"I certainly think it is not surprising for a child to eat compulsively following both neglect and sexual trauma," Emma explained. "We know that she was food deprived in her birth home."

"Yes, but the Greens say this didn't happen when they had her," Roxie said.

"OK, yes," Emma continued. "But a three-year-old is really starting to feed themselves and realize their own capacity to alter their state of hunger. It makes sense to me that this might show up later once she can access food herself instead of being fed by a caretaker. This girl has been through so much, I think we will see all kinds of symptoms as we work through trauma. And Roxie, think about the trauma of having to perform oral sex at her age. I mean, you know, the psychodynamic implications."

"OK, I see, yes," Roxie responded. "And I certainly don't believe that was the only incident. There had to be some grooming going on for quite a while. It's hard to believe the first incident was that severe. But she has been losing weight. We can't let her get too underweight."

"I agree," Emma said. "Maybe you could kind of ask Ms. Lee a little about it. Either subtly or directly. Or, when you have been there, have you seen the kids eating or smelled food being cooked?"

"I haven't," Roxie stated. "But I can sure ask about it."

Visiting Grandma

Deja climbed up on Ms. Lee's lap while Roxie got her notebook and pen from her bag. Ms. Lee kissed her on the top of her head and said, "You know Grandma loves you." Deja giggled and kissed Ms. Lee on the cheek.

She always looks like she is dressed for church on Sunday, Roxie thought. Ms. Lee always had well styled hair, painted nails, wore dresses and makeup, and sat calmly with her legs crossed.

"Ms. Lee," Roxie began, "I am always so impressed with how clean your house is. Even the kids' rooms!"

"Oh, goodness," Ms. Lee laughed. "The kids are all such good helpers. We all have to pick up with this many kiddos in the house!"

Deja jumped off Ms. Lee's lap and ran to get a stuffed rabbit to show Roxie.

"She's sure proud of that new bunny," Ms. Lee exclaimed as Roxie played with Deja. Deja hopped the rabbit towards the dining room. She sat it in a small chair at a kid sized table next to the larger dining room table. *Cute.* Roxie thought. *An easy to clean dining table for the little ones since the bigger table just has four chairs.*

"Is that where your rabbit has dinner, Deja?" Roxie asked. The little girl nodded. "Do you have dinner here with your rabbit?" Deja smiled and nodded, sitting down by the rabbit in one of the other chairs.

"You know, Ms. Lee," Roxie continued. "I am usually here around lunchtime. But I wonder why your house never smells like food? I mean, it smells like super clean in here. Like you just finished polishing all the furniture!"

Ms. Lee was silent.

"Are you sayin' I didn't, that I don't feed these kids?" She said slowly. Her voice was lower, and her forehead creased.

"No," Roxie said calmly. "But it is my job to ask and make sure."

"I fix sandwiches for lunch. They like ham sandwiches. You got a problem with that?" Ms. Lee's face had clouded over.

"No," Roxie continued. "That is fine. But the other foster family has been raising concerns that Deja is losing weight. I am just checking it out."

"Oh yeah? They think they got room to criticize me? And she's a picky little eater, did they tell you that? And I have lots of kids and I can't be making a special meal for each one every day." Ms. Lee responded, her voice becoming louder. "Let me show you something." She loudly opened and closed a drawer.

"Look at this," she said jabbing her finger at a chart in front of Roxie. "WIC gave me this and she's just fine on this chart." Roxie looked at the chart and confirmed that while Deja was slightly underweight for her height and age, it did not look alarming.

"Thanks for showing me that," Roxie said, genuinely. "I am so glad to see that Deja is on track on the charts, and that you are taking care of her."

Ms. Lee seemed to relax and returned to her chair.

"And you know what I just remembered, Ms. Lee?" Roxie wondered aloud. "I remember the other family took her to a doctor who put her on Ritalin. Is she still taking that?" *How could I forget that? They wanted a 3-year-old child on Ritalin. But people lose weight on that and who knows what it might do to a 3-year-old?*

"I give her all the medicine I am supposed to," Ms. Lee said. "I am doing just fine with her."

"I know, I understand," Roxie nodded. "Thank you for answering those questions."

"It's fine, Miss Roxie," Ms. Lee said kindly. "I know you have to ask all kinds of things. I just feel so angry at those other people for letting their boy hurt Deja. I just can't imagine someone doing that and then acting like I am the one not treating her right."

Ms. Lee smiled warmly as they wrapped up the visit and she held the door open for Roxie. Deja hugged Ms. Lee's leg as they stood in the doorway.

Roxie processed the events in her mind as she walked to her car. *With the trauma and the meds, this does make some sense. But Ms. Lee seemed so different, maybe defensive? But really, who wouldn't be? She has done all of this work helping children and she probably felt pretty unappreciated. But I know the Greens are going to keep making these accusations and trying to get Deja back. I sure don't want to advocate for the wrong family. How can I sort out what is true here?*

3   Who Belongs?

Diane felt her blood pressure rising as conflict mounted in the meeting.

Dr. Paul spoke up forcefully, "We came tonight representing our church that has been considering joining Austin Interfaith. But now I need some clarification about what this organization stands for. As Christians, we cannot and will not condone homosexuality. What is Austin Interfaith's position on that?"

Joseph, the lead organizer for Austin Interfaith, was not able to remain silent any longer. He quickly replied, "We don't ever take a position that is against any member institution's core beliefs."

Before anyone else could comment, Greg burst out, "If you aren't going to support us, why should we support you? Our core beliefs require full inclusion of all regardless of sexual orientation." He got up, pulled Louise to her feet, and the two of them angrily left the meeting. As the pastor of Greg and Louise's church, Diane sat in stunned silence trying to determine her next move.

Diane

Diane was a white woman who grew up in Oklahoma City. People gravitated towards her caring attitude and welcoming smile. Since childhood, Diane had been sensitive to the sorrows and longings of others, often serving as the friend who encouraged, sympathized, and advocated for those in need. In college, she learned that the pattern of pouring herself out for others while often neglecting her own needs was not healthy, but also not unusual.

Diane earned her BSW from The University of Texas at Arlington. After graduation, she worked at a hospital, doing discharge planning. Social work was satisfying at first, but she felt restless sometimes and curious about whether she was being called to congregational ministry. At dinner one night, she told her husband, "I really like the part of my job that's helping people. When I get to work closely with patients and their families, my work feels meaningful. Today when one family was sharing about their experience, they started talking about their church and faith in God. I wanted to talk with them about scripture and prayer, too. Moments like this keep coming up; I wonder if I should go into pastoral ministry. I am thinking seriously about applying to go to seminary."

Soon Diane enrolled in the Brite Divinity School in Fort Worth to earn a Master of Divinity degree. There she began learning about community organizing. She was inspired by the way that community organizing united groups that usually did not collaborate well with one another and were able to work on common issues such as public education and criminal justice reform.

After graduating from Brite, Diane divorced and moved to Austin to pastor a progressive, non-denominational congregation, Flores Christian. Diane's journey towards ordained pastoral ministry wove together different strands of her education, social work, and community service; that all converged when the congregation she pastored joined other congregations in community organizing with Austin Interfaith. When conflicts erupted within her congregation, she thought back to that time when she considered a career change and wondered if she should have remained in social work. But more often, Diane was deeply satisfied how different aspects of her vocation all fit together.

Austin Interfaith

Austin Interfaith (AI) was founded in the 1980s. As an Industrial Areas Foundation (IAF) affiliate, AI used the skills of broad-based organizing to develop leadership, identify issues, reweave relationships, and build the capacity within member institutions to act on issues that affected their constituent leaders. Members of IAF affiliates were institutions, and AI's members included a variety of congregations, schools, and unions. Leaders engaged in one-on-one relational meetings, small group conversations called "house meetings," neighborhood and community walks, and research actions.

Joseph Washington was the paid, professional, lead organizer of AI, and an ordained African Methodist Episcopal Church (AME) minister. He had 11 years of experience as an IAF organizer, and was married to a social worker. In workshops he often reminded leaders, "Organizing is *always* connected to the missions of our institutions, and should be flexible in order to meet the needs of each congregation or school. Our actions are always followed by reflection so that we can learn from both our successes and mistakes. Our business is the development and formation of people."

Flores Christian was actively engaged in AI. Diane's church members had been inspired by attending an accountability session with public officials and candidates who were publicly invited to go on record on a variety of concerns including increasing funding for public transportation in the state budget. Several members of Diane's congregation often relied on the public bus system to get to work and church. Diane encouraged them to meet with leaders from other AI institutions exploring actions related to public transportation.

Austin, Texas

Austin was the state capital of Texas and home to the University of Texas at Austin (one of the biggest universities in the U.S.). Austin had grown exponentially over the past few decades due to an influx of high-tech industry, and the U.S. News and World Report named Austin the best place to live in 2017 and 2018. As wealthy people moved in from out of state, gentrification and affordable housing became large problems for Austin. And as the city grew, so did traffic congestion, but public transit did not.

When they first met, Joseph told Diane, "Austin may be the most progressive city in the state, but it's just a veneer. I've been discriminated against here and you will hear lots of stories like this in Austin Interfaith."

Flores Christian and members

Diane often told people, "My congregation is the best church in the region! I am so proud and thankful to be their pastor." Members of Flores Christian inspired her by extravagant acts of compassion and care for some of the most vulnerable people in their community. The congregation had formed when a small group was asked to leave another congregation because of conflict over inclusion of gays and lesbians. Although the small church struggled financially, they shared a wealth of prophetic social activism, generosity of service and spirit, and inclusive hospitality. Half a dozen of the founding members were gay men living with HIV/AIDS, and five of them had died during the first few years after the congregations formed. But, new members joined. Some of them were young families who wanted to raise their children with inclusive values. Some had family members who were lesbian or gay. Although about half of the regular members identified as queer, transgender, intersex, lesbian, gay, or bisexual persons, many members were heterosexual people who believed that sexual orientation should not be a barrier to full inclusion.

Diane had been their pastor for five years now, and she hoped to continue in that position for many more years. Sometimes the high-level conflict surrounding her work as an openly bisexual pastor was tiring, and Diane began to consider getting more training to become an IAF organizer. Her theology was so liberal that she sometimes wondered if she belonged in the pastoral ministry at all.

She was especially impressed with the leadership development she saw in various members of her congregation who participated with AI. For example, Louise was a 50-year-old without a high school diploma who worked in the communication industry. She struggled to pay her bills as a single person who was paid 12 dollars an hour. Because her old car was unreliable, Louise often used the public bus system. Louise was respected and loved as a church leader in the congregation, but had experienced discrimination in the past. Participating in the AI transportation action team was a big step for Louise. Before she got involved, she asked Diane, "Will leaders from other churches accept me as a lesbian? Should I avoid mentioning that I'm gay?"

Diane knew that as an African American in a Southern city, Louise's decision to come out as a lesbian had not been easy. Although her adult sons and her mother all accepted her, other members of her extended family were critical. Louise told Diane, "I'm convinced that my supervisor at work and several co-workers are uncomfortable because of my sexual orientation as well. But I'm not leaving." Diane knew that good jobs were difficult to find given Louise's age and level of education. Diane wondered how the AI leaders would react to Louise. Both women were relieved when Louise was welcomed and accepted in the transportation action team. Flores was committed to community organizing and was proud to be a dues-paying institutional member.

Then came a day when Diane got a call from Louise. "I have breast cancer. It's going to be tough, but I'm grateful that I have my church friends."

"I hope you know that you can count on the congregation to circle around you during this difficult time," Diane said. "You've been a stalwart leader in this church for many years. You've ministered on care teams for friends living with HIV/AIDS. I think people will be glad to give back to you."

"Thanks, Pastor Diane," Louise said. "I know I can trust friends from church, especially Greg. He is my best friend. We've been singing in the choir together for years. Please keep praying for me."

Nevertheless, Diane was anxious about both Louise's financial and physical health future. She had witnessed the radical hospitality and generosity of the people in the Flores Christian family of faith, but wasn't sure that would be enough help for Louise.

Because of all the responsibilities she had to juggle, Diane struggled to keep in close contact with Louise about her illness and treatment. She knew Louise needed help accessing services and managing as a single person. Her past training and experience as a social worker were good assets in situations like this that often emerged in congregational life. Members of the congregation kept reaching out to Louise even when her health declined and she attended church less often. Louise's friend, Greg, called Diane often to ask about possible support services for Louise. Diane remembered that AI had a team investigating health care issues and possible actions to improve access to health care. Diane asked Greg to come with her to the next AI health care meeting. Greg mentioned to Louise that they planned to attend. The three of them decided to try attending that meeting together.

On the day of the meeting, Greg called Diane in the morning.

"Hey Pastor," Greg said. "How recently have you talked with Louise?"

Diane acknowledged to herself that her first impulse was to feel a little defensive and guilty because it had been one of those weeks when she had not found time yet to visit with Louise or even call. "I haven't talked with her this week," she replied.

"I have been worrying more and more about Louise living alone. I knew that her boss had been pressuring her to leave her job because of increasing absences and declining abilities. She told me yesterday was her last day at work. I wasn't surprised because she is spending more and more time in bed recently. The big problem is that now she has no health insurance at all. What she did have through work wasn't great, but at least it was something. She doesn't qualify for Medicaid yet due to her income this year."

Diane knew that besides Greg, Sally, Harold, and a few other volunteers from church had been going by from time to time to visit Louise. "How much longer do you think Louise can live alone?"

"Her family can't really take off work much without compromising their own job security. Her mother is in a nursing home unable to help. She seems to be depending more and more on the few visits from home health care assistants paid for by the state. I am hoping that some of our friends from the AI health care action team could help. I want to ask them tonight at the meeting to see who else might provide some care," Greg said.

Diane knew that providing direct services like care was not the focus of AI. But, she felt grieved and powerless to respond to all these needs. She wondered whether she could add a regular afternoon each week to sit with Louise, or help out more herself. Sighing heavily, Diane told Greg, "I want to do everything we can to support Louise during this process. I'm not sure how much help AI can be, but let's see if we can find new ways to support Louise at the AI meeting."

The Meeting

Greg gave Louise a ride to the evening meeting of the AI health care action team; they arrived ten minutes early. Joseph was meeting with Terry, the AI leader who would chair the meeting that night. Terry and Joseph greeted Louise and Greg warmly, and explained that they were reviewing the agenda they had created together for the meeting. Diane arrived a few minutes later and sat with Greg and Louise. Diane had been to enough of these meetings to know Terry, Joseph, and several other leaders. Before long, about a dozen additional people drifted in and filled the seats around the large table. The meeting began with an opening prayer and a round of introductions. Diane was glad to see that Louise was not the only person of color in the room. Four African American leaders introduced themselves as being from a Baptist church that was an institutional member of AI. Most of the participants belonged to institutions like schools or congregations that were officially AI members. However, there were two people from a Nazarene church that was considering joining. In contrast to other leaders that evening, these visitors were wearing suits and ties.

Terry led the meeting with patience and skill. Diane watched with interest, noticing the progress of competencies these leaders were developing. The group was considering possible actions related to Medicaid expansion in their state. Several leaders joined Terry in reporting on the research they had been conducting to understand various players who had interest in the local health care system.

One of the visitors, Dr. Paul, was a white physician with important connections in the city. Diane felt guilty at her own discomfort around Dr. Paul, whom she knew from other public settings; she thought, *He's got a socially conservative agenda that represents many problems in our community. But I know AI believes in diversity, so I'll try to keep an open mind.* When the group broke into pairs for one-on-one meetings, Greg met with one of the leaders of the Baptist church, and Louise met with a Unitarian leader named Steve. Diane tried to move towards Dr. Paul to introduce herself, but he turned to another man sitting nearby. Diane felt a little relieved and met with a leader of a Roman Catholic parish instead.

One-on-one meetings, sometimes called individual meetings, were a tool Diane appreciated from the AI training she had received up to that point. She appreciated the capacity to listen more deeply with focused attention. By awakening more fully to the power of curiosity and wonder, the AI training helped Diane develop her own spirituality and leadership capabilities. Although most individual meetings would not be conducted in a room with many other people competing to hear each other, AI meetings typically did include some time to break into pairs and practice individual meetings. Like her previous experiences with this practice, Diane bonded with the new friend she met that evening. Working more closely as public allies with people who were from other faith traditions or secular institutions enhanced Diane's own faith journey.

While she shared conversation during that individual meeting, Diane couldn't help but overhear bits of the communication of other pairs around her in the room. She saw that Louise was choking back tears sharing about her situation with a man who listened with intense concern. She overheard Dr. Paul saying something about scripture and witness. Diane worked to redirect her own attention back to the woman in front of her, and mentioned how impressed she was with the theological diversity in the organization.

After 15 minutes, Terry announced, "OK, let's come back together as an entire group to discuss how the individual meetings went. Let's hear your reactions to your individual meetings." Several pairs were having such animated conversations that it took a few moments to shift back to the meeting. Steve, who had met with Louise, burst out with clear passion, "We need to recruit some people to help Louise with her care team. Her story is heartbreaking! If she was white and heterosexual, the health care system would be more responsive to her."

The room hummed with a potent silence for about ten seconds. Terry, who was chairing the meeting, tried to decide how to respond. *Didn't everyone in the meeting understand that volunteering for a care team was not the type of thing AI did?* Diane wondered.

Joseph waited to see if the leaders would steer the group through this slight logjam. Diane thought, *Our iron rule is "Never do things for people that they can do for themselves." But shouldn't Joseph step in here?*

Diane hoped her voice sounded calmer than she felt as she ventured to speak up to the group.

"I know that AI is not like a charity that provides direct services, but in this situation, Louise cannot do many things for herself during her illness. Where is the balance? Wouldn't this be an opportunity for us to collaborate together?"

Greg jumped in and said, "I came tonight hoping that some of you could help our congregation support Louise. We are a small church, and we only have a limited number of volunteers to help with all her needs. Or maybe the health care team take up a collection for Louise?"

Louise spoke up next, "Actually, I was thinking about doing a sit-in at the health clinic and trying to get some media attention through getting arrested. People like me who lose their insurance illustrate some of the problems in the health care system. This could generate some great publicity for Austin Interfaith, I can see the headlines now: Black Lesbian Cancer Patient Needs Health Care." Louise looked more energized than she had looked in months.

Greg replied with enthusiasm, "Great, we can get the Equality Texas and the ACLU involved!" Diane knew that Greg had participated in many public protest actions before. She could see that he was getting excited about the possibilities. Diane noticed that some of the people in the meeting had troubled expressions on their faces and were shifting uneasily in their seats.

Terry tried again to regain control of the meeting, saying, "Let's come back to those questions after hearing from everyone about how their individual meetings went." An awkward pause followed. Diane wondered how Greg and Louise felt about the direction of the meeting. She knew that AI's mission was to develop and organize leaders to take action for advocacy to change policy, not provide direct services, and that protests and sit-ins were not the first line of action. Diane waited to see how the rest of the meeting would unfold. She desperately wanted her congregation to continue its strong interest in AI. At the same time, her pastor's heart ached for Greg and Louise who looked as if their hopes were dashed in that moment.

But before the group was able to move on, Dr. Paul, one of the visitors from the Nazarene church spoke up forcefully, "We came tonight representing our congregation that has been considering joining AI. But, now I need some clarification about what this organization stands for. As Christians, we do not and will not condone homosexuality. What is AI's position on that?" Some faces around the room looked stunned.

Joseph was not able to remain silent any longer. He quickly replied, "We don't ever take a position that is against any member institution's core beliefs." As the lead organizer, Joseph was responsible for overseeing the strength of the whole AI organization, including bringing in new institutions and raising financial resources. Joseph looked from Dr. Paul's red face to Terry's dazed expression.

Terry said, "AI needs a broad diversity of denominations and institutions to build healthy and effective networks and accomplish our shared agenda. We are really hoping that your church will join, Dr. Paul."

Diane thought, *This is a level of conflict I experience with overseeing my congregation and its controversial position in the public life of the community. It's not very different from the tension in community organizing. But I still don't like conflict.* She glanced anxiously at Louise and Greg to see how they were responding, and found herself scrambling internally to settle the questions of how to explain the importance of her congregation's core beliefs in this public setting. *We're not a congregation united by a creed or set of doctrine in the same way that many congregations are; members of our church have diverse views and opinions themselves. It's always difficult for others to understand who we are. But how can AI collaborate with churches that could not affirm the full equality and sacred dignity of LGBTQ members?*

Before anyone else could comment, Greg burst out, "If you aren't going to support us, why should we support you? Our core beliefs require full inclusion of all regardless of sexual orientation." He got up, pulled Louise to her feet, and the two of them left the meeting.

Diane didn't move. She looked at Joseph and then Terry. Did she belong in this room or not?

Part II
Master of Social Work Practicum Students

4 All for Love

Sean stepped off the sagging porch steps and began walking down the driveway. As he stepped into his car, he looked back at the group of four that had gathered on the porch to see him off.

Robert had a huge smile, waving enthusiastically, with his other arm around Melinda's shoulders. Melinda looked down, maybe at the ground or at a stain on her nightgown. Nick had turned to go inside, and Jessie stared intently at Sean with her hand on her hip.

Melinda is a vulnerable adult here, Sean thought, *but anything I might do to protect her would separate her from Robert. I want to make sure she is safe, but I also want to respect that Melinda and Robert deserve to have a relationship. I sure don't want to be another part of the system just rolling over people.*

Life in Fayetteville

As the third largest city in Arkansas, Fayetteville had plenty of the bustle of a city, but maintained a college feel. Football fans gathered to watch the Arkansas Razorbacks play, and tourists often visited the historic home of Bill and Hillary Clinton. But the poverty rate in Fayetteville ranked above the national average, and the services for low income people with disabilities were ranked poorly. The main industries of the area, Wal-Mart and Tyson chicken, employed workers at low wages while the University of Arkansas provided more prestigious employment.

The Adult Protective Services of Arkansas

Adult Protective Services (APS), part of the Department of Human Services (DHS), had a mission to investigate suspected abuse, neglect, and exploitation of vulnerable adults. While many services were provided in protection for the elderly and in response to elder abuse, APS also investigated cases involving adults with mental illnesses or developmental disabilities that created significant vulnerability.

Referrals usually came from the community or from other service providers who were concerned about the environment of an adult. APS would send the Adult Specialist, sometimes in a team and sometimes alone, to perform a needs assessment, a risk assessment, and do a brief screen for capacity referred to as the "Clox" assessment: a simple analog clock drawing test designed to measure executive function. The Adult Specialist also assessed for orientation, signs of psychosis, further indicators of dementia, or evidence of a cognitive disability.

Assessments always involved evaluation of the home, but the paradigm was somewhat different for adults than for assessing the environment for children. The main focus was if the home was functional. The home needed to have working utilities and access to all the rooms, but many homes that were severely neglected or dirty might still be considered functional enough to not require intervention. As long as the person was ambulatory and able to obtain food on their own, DHS did not require that a home be stocked with food.

Before removing a client from a harmful situation, the Adult Specialist had two determinations to make during an assessment: the client must lack capacity and there must be evidence of abuse, neglect, or exploitation that could result in serious physical harm and/or major financial loss. If these conditions were present, the Adult Specialist, with the cooperation of a Supervisor, initiated a process of contacting the DHS legal team to help secure emergency guardianship. The process of staffing the case, petitioning the judge for guardianship, and appearing in court could take up to a week.

One of the biggest obstacles to overcome during the process of securing guardianship was establishing where a client would be placed following the guardianship hearing. The APS Supervisor would not allow a guardianship petition to go forward unless there was a facility willing to accept the client immediately after the hearing. The judge, also, was historically resistant to granting state guardianships without a placement facility lined up to provide care for the client. Typically, there was no way to ensure a resolution to the substantiated abuse, neglect, or exploitation without relying on a care facility to take over the care of the vulnerable adult.

The APS Supervisor helped the Specialist sort through the information to make decisions about whether the abuse or neglect allegations are substantiated, but the Supervisor often depended solely on the judgment of the Specialist when it came to determining capacity and the severity of the maltreatment. The Supervisor rarely took a role in making the decision for the Specialist on whether or not to pursue guardianship, realizing that the Specialist had the first-hand knowledge from visiting the client and the role of supervision was more to collaborate and guide.

APS clients were most commonly placed in nursing homes if they were physically disabled or lived with advanced dementia and were placed in residential care facilities if they were primarily cognitively disabled or severely mentally ill. Guardianships were very labor-intensive for the Specialist, were often irreversible, and always placed a client's health and safety above individual wishes.

Sean Martin, Adult Protective Services Specialist

Sean Martin was a multiracial man in his 30s, whose beard and glasses gave him a studious look. After working at a bookstore for several years and earning a bachelor's degree in English, he decided he wanted a career where he could focus on helping the disadvantaged in his community. He heard of the APS job at DHS in 2007, without knowing many of the details, but thought it sounded like a meaningful way to help disabled people live better lives. After beginning the job, he quickly learned he enjoyed the human interactions the job required. He loved the whole idea of going to a stranger's house, knocking on the door, and just getting to know a person he might otherwise never have met. He observed that his clients had no other access to support and seemed to be on a "social island." *When I step into their lives, they're right on the edge of either disaster or a major life change,* he often thought. *There's no telling what's going to happen, and I may or may not be able to help them, but I like that they're adults and I don't necessarily have to make decisions for them. We can just talk about it and work on solving problems together. I like that I get to treat people as equals, when other people in their lives completely ostracize them. It is magical in a way, a gift, to get to step in to someone's life like that and try to be helpful.*

He loved his work, but also loved learning, reading, and growing intellectually and professionally. Soon his wife encouraged him to pursue his MSW, and he began the MSW program at the University of Arkansas in 2014. He attended classes on a part-time schedule so he could continue working at DHS and spend time with his wife and elementary school age son. As Sean started his final practicum in 2017, his family grew larger with the arrival of a second child, so Sean now juggled his practicum demands, employment, course work, and the challenges of his growing family.

Sean's practicum was employment based at APS, providing solution-focused therapy to some of the clients served by APS that could benefit from therapeutic intervention. While he continued his work as an Adult Specialist, if he determined clients were a good candidate for therapy, he could offer them that service and arrange to see them in their homes. The therapy clients could be seen separately and count for his practicum experience.

Meeting Robert at the Crisis Center

Sean first met Robert Garrison in January, responding to a report to APS that an intellectually disabled man with an approximate intellectual functioning of a 7-year-old was brought to the crisis center by the police. Upon arriving at the crisis center, he was updated by the nurse who had made the referral alleging self-neglect.

"The police said they had received calls about a white man 'displaying himself' outside the Walgreens store over on Hudson street," began Rita Barnes, RN, using air quotes when referring to the indecent exposure. She walked Sean through the hallways of the unit back to the client meeting area.

"And when they arrived they found Robert asleep on the sidewalk with his pants around his knees," the nurse continued. "They brought him here for a mental health evaluation where he admitted to using meth. We called APS with the hope that you all could figure out a placement before his discharge." She looked at Sean with a hopeful expression.

Sean immediately had a sinking feeling, realizing how unlikely a client with Robert's history would be accepted into a group home. *Supportive housing placements for clients with intellectual disabilities are difficult to find*, he thought, *much less for clients with sexual acting out behaviors and drug use. And the state facilities for the developmentally disabled often have a ten-year waiting list!*

Sean met with Robert at the center and assessed his needs. Robert was a tall, strong looking man who made large gestures and had a bright affect. Sean observed that Robert was affable and enthusiastic, with a broad smile, seeming to welcome the opportunity to meet a new person.

"Robert," Sean had asked frankly towards the end of the interview, "what would you like to do when you leave the crisis center?"

Robert shrugged and smiled.

"What options do you see for where you can live when you leave?" Sean asked. "Is there somewhere you have in mind, or are you wanting me to help you find a group home placement?"

"I don't want a group home," Robert had said, "But it's ok, I have lots of places I can go, I don't mind."

"I want to follow up with you wherever you go," Sean said, "and I want you to let me set you up with a payee from an agency in town. They can help you get control of your disability check and also help your chances of finding housing."

"No way," Robert stated emphatically. "I will never use a payee again—they only steal my money or force me to do things with them to get my money."

I don't know if that is a delusion or true, but it isn't surprising as sometimes those situations occur when clients don't utilize a professional as their payee, Sean thought. *But it doesn't sound like he is likely to accept a payee from an agency as part of the solution right now.*

Sean called several places hoping to find a placement option that he might be able to present to Robert. He continued to see Robert and keep in touch with the crisis center over the next few days, but Sean was soon informed by the crisis center that Robert had been discharged "to the street." Sean called the local shelters, but eventually had to accept that there was not a way to find Robert and that there was not much he could do to help for now.

Meeting Melinda at the Shelter

As Sean's practicum progressed into February, he responded to a referral regarding Melinda Wolfe, age 24, at the homeless shelter. He stopped at the case management office to get a visitor's badge and meet Melinda's case manager, Elizabeth Mitchell.

"Melinda's intellectually disabled and according to her grandmother, she has been guessed to function about like an 8-year-old," Elizabeth said. "She'd been living with her grandmother and it was, well, it got pretty verbally hostile with her grandmother, and that resulted in the apartment manager banning Melinda from the property and the grandmother got a protective order. Melinda showed up here yesterday, and we called Grandma. She says

Melinda has Autism too, so maybe that explains it, but she's pretty difficult to get talking."

Elizabeth entered the commons area while Sean took a seat in the small room used for meeting with clients. Soon, Elizabeth returned with a young woman with long dark hair. Elizabeth made the introductions and left as Melinda took a seat across from Sean.

Realizing Melinda was new to the shelter and likely very afraid, Sean spent time trying to build rapport with Melinda. But her affect remained very flat, her answers brief, and she rarely looked up from staring at the floor.

"So on one hand you sure don't like it here at the shelter, but on the other hand you aren't sure if a group home sounds good either?" Sean questioned after the topic of next steps for housing arose, trying to summarize what Melinda had expressed.

"I don't care where I end up," Melinda answered quietly.

"You don't care if you end up staying here at the shelter a long time?" Sean reflected.

"Well, it's okay until I get the baby," Melinda responded with a quick flash of eye contact before returning her gaze to her shoes. "My friend has a baby and she said that someday she'd just give me the baby so I'll need a place to live then."

"OK," Sean responded, a little surprised. "I guess we need to think about the best way to get ready for that." *That was a strange comment that may not even be true*, he thought, *but since it seems like a dream in the future instead of something actually happening right now, maybe it will motivate her to find and maintain housing.*

He continued meeting with Melinda, but she dropped the subject of the baby very quickly. However, Sean soon discovered a large obstacle in regard to group home placement; Melinda did not receive a disability check, and therefore did not have Medicaid or any other source of payment that would allow her to obtain placement. Her grandmother had provided for her financially, even though Melinda was likely to qualify for disability. But that left her now without an income, medical coverage, and no clear options for housing outside of the shelter. After the interview, Sean briefed Elizabeth who stated she would begin immediately helping Melinda apply for disability benefits.

"We have the legal aid folks here every week," Elizabeth informed Sean. "I don't know how long it will take to get things rolling, but I think we can handle it here faster than anyone else." Sean agreed and told Elizabeth he would start looking for potential placement options to consider once the disability was approved and they could coordinate as needed. But again, he left feeling there was little he could do at that time.

Home Visit with the Happy Couple

A couple months later, Sean received a referral from a street outreach preacher, known locally as Pastor Vick.

"His name's Rob Garrison," the pastor explained, "and he's been homeless but he's moved into this new house and the situation is just terrible. Just awful. There's drugs there, the house is plain disgusting, and it's just very dangerous for him. He needs your help right away."

Robert! Sean thought. *Great! While this situation does not sound good, it is good to have a new call and location so I can go follow up and see how he is doing. Maybe now there is more I can do to help.*

The next day, Sean drove up to the house noting its poor condition, standing out as dilapidated even in a neighborhood of other neglected homes. He saw Robert sitting on the porch.

"Sean!" Robert shouted with animation, immediately recognizing Sean. He jumped to his feet and held out his hand for Sean to shake. Robert had a big smile and seemed very excited.

"Good to see you, Robert," Sean answered warmly. "Last time I saw you it was at the crisis center. I knew you were back on the streets after that, but looks like you have other arrangements now?" Sean noted that Robert was wearing clothes that while not perfectly clean, were not troublingly dirty. He looked disheveled and was unshaven and sweaty, but like he was able to attend to hygiene on a basic level.

Sean and Robert both took a seat on the porch steps. Robert was hunched over and looked down but remained animated. Sean noted a smell of urine and decided it was coming from the house, not from Robert himself.

"I met a girl," Robert said excitedly. "Melinda. We're engaged! We want to start a family. But we were at the shelter and did not want to be at the shelter so we came here."

"You met Melinda at the shelter?" Sean asked. *Melinda that was my client too?* he wondered. *What a coincidence it would be if these two people found each other at the shelter and got all googly eyed and ran with it.*

"Yes! But she did not want to be there, she did not like it. It was not good for her there. She is not used to things like that and did not want to stay there. But we met Nick and Jessie and they are very nice to us. They let us stay in this house and Nick helps me take care of my money so I can someday get a place with Melinda and we can have a baby."

A child would go straight to child welfare, Sean thought sadly. *As much as they would love the child, they don't appear capable of independent living themselves, much less able to raise a child. They have no family support and no resources to help them be successful. I wish they could, but it would probably be a painful situation. But I hate thinking that way.*

"Nick is your payee? Your check is going to him now?" Sean questioned. "You were dead set against a payee last time we talked. I really want to encourage you to get a payee from The Center for Disabled Adults, Robert. They have lots of people there who could really be trusted to take care of your money. You wouldn't have to worry about someone taking off with it or any other problems."

"Nick can do it! He is very nice to me," Robert responded. "They're not gonna steal my money like other folks have, they're not. They want to help us. Help us get a place. Get a place of our own. They know we need our money."

"Robert, I know with some of your payees in the past," Sean began.

"I know!" Robert interrupted. "I know I've said before about all the stuff, but not here. Here I only have sex with my girlfriend and it's ok because we're engaged. That's all, just her."

Sean had his doubts, and lots of questions in his mind about this payee situation, drugs, the relationship with Melinda, housing, and a million other things. But he wanted to focus on the current situation of safe housing for now.

"OK, Robert. We can talk more about all that later, and I'd like to meet Nick and check out that he knows what his responsibilities are as a payee."

"Sure!" Robert said loudly.

"Robert, does Nick have a way that he earns his own money?" Sean asked.

"Sure, he fixes cars. His friends come over and work with him and they fix cars together sometimes. Here in the driveway, they fix cars."

"Do you know if anyone here uses drugs or alcohol?" Sean asked frankly.

"Well, Nick does sometimes I think," Robert began. "But just because sometimes he needs a little bit of extra energy so he can stay up all night and take care of Jessie because she feels sick sometimes and needs him. But just a little. And not me."

"OK," Sean responded thoughtfully. *Is there meth in this house?* Sean wondered. *Is Robert using it and not wanting to tell me? This Nick guy might be using him for his disability check and apparently is using meth, but Robert is his own guardian.* By now, the smell of urine was stronger and Sean suspected it was from several different animals.

"Robert," Sean continued, "how about you show me around inside and let me meet everybody?"

As Robert opened the door and led him inside, Sean was overwhelmed by the smell. He smelled different kinds of urine and feces, guessing it was mostly from cats, and a sour, mildewy, trash smell. He saw piles of empty fast food containers, bottles, other trash and dirty clothes all over the floor and numerous piles of cat feces. He carefully began to walk around the room, avoiding stepping in feces. He walked towards the kitchen passing a sagging, damaged couch and noticed larger feces, maybe from a dog.

Sean flipped a light switch and was surprised to see that the electricity was working. He looked down at his feet and the dirty carpet where about ten large roaches scattered in reaction to the light. Most of the floor was either covered in papers or clothes, but he also saw some wet spots around piles of feces. *That doesn't even look like a urine spot*, he thought. *It's more like the feces swelled up and is in a pool of liquid.*

"Robert," Sean asked. "Does the water work?"

"Sure," Robert said, and turned on the kitchen tap.

"That's great, Robert," Sean said. "And can I see if you have food in the fridge and the pantry? I just want to check out if you have what you need. It's no fun being hungry."

"We don't got much," Robert said as he opened the refrigerator door. The refrigerator was mostly empty except for cans of beer, bottles of ketchup and mustard, a few fast food sacks, and a partial loaf of bread.

"Where do you keep food that doesn't need the fridge?" Sean asked.

Robert opened a cupboard where Sean saw a couple cans of soup, some noodles, and a jar of peanut butter. Sean counted four roaches in the cupboard.

"Thanks, Robert," Sean said. Robert's face lit up and Sean turned to see what he was looking at.

"Melinda!" Robert shouted loudly. "Sean, Melinda's here!"

Sean extended his hand to greet her, noting that she was indeed the Melinda he had met in the past. She was also slightly disheveled and wore a dirty nightgown. He had a brief moment of wondering about confidentiality and how to greet her, but luckily she took care of the situation.

"I know you," she said flatly, nodding. "I still don't got my disability."

"Oh, I hope it comes through soon," Sean responded. "And I am really glad to see you. I remember the case manager at the shelter was helping you with that so that you could go to the group home."

"I got Robert now," she stated, still flat but making eye contact. *She seems more comfortable, more relaxed than she was at the shelter*, Sean thought.

"We're living here and we're engaged and we want to start a family. It's good here, nothing bad happens here. It's a lot better than the homeless shelter, I'm glad I'm not there anymore," Melinda stated. "It's kind of like I can be me now, like now that I'm away from Gramma and after being homeless and all, I kind of get to start over here and be me." She smiled slightly.

That was more talkative than she has ever been, Sean thought. He asked her more questions about the living situation, including if there were drugs in the home, which she denied. The smell in the home was overpowering, making it difficult to breathe. The acrid, suffocating smell of urine seemed stronger the longer Sean was in the home.

A thin man, maybe Hispanic and in his early 30s, walked through the door with a tall, large white woman. *This must be Nick and Jessie*, Sean thought. Nick looked intently and silently at Sean, but Jessie was friendly and began talking rapidly and without pause.

"You must be here to talk to Robert and Melinda," Jessie began. "It is so great to have them here, we're taking real good care of them. You know I don't mind them here because it's good for us all and they are just doing great with us, no worries. We're just so glad to see them out of the shelter, that place isn't good for anyone. It's loud and there are just so many people there you never know what's gonna happen, but they sure do like it here with us."

Jessie continued, but Sean moved towards the door, hoping to encourage Nick and Jessie to follow him outside so he could speak to them alone. *I want to make sure Nick and Jessie know about their responsibilities, and maybe instill a little fear in them, about what the legal consequences will be if they allow harm to occur to disabled adults, and the legal consequences of exploiting their money. But I don't want to create a bunch of fear and confusion for Robert and Melinda.* But unable to separate the couples, he asked Nick if he understood the responsibilities of being a payee in front of the whole group.

"We can do all that, there is no problem here," Nick repeated after most all of Sean's questions and explanations about being a payee. He too denied that there were drugs in the home.

"No," Nick said making eye contact with Sean and speaking slowly. "No drugs."

I am not sure about this guy, Sean thought. *Sometimes people are the payee for their kin or someone they care about, but it is pretty strange for this to be just out of the goodness of his heart for a person he just met.*

"Are Robert and Melinda here alone most of the time?" Sean asked.

"Yeah, they do a lot around the house, and I mean they live here too so we don't get in each other's way," Nick answered. "Are we about done here?" Nick asked, raising his eyebrows. He put his hand on the doorknob, leading Sean out.

They need supervision! Sean thought urgently. *Melinda has so little experience with being homeless and is so vulnerable to maltreatment. She is not someone who can survive well homeless or on the streets. And Robert has a history of falling victim to all kinds of exploitation, and I don't want either one of them around drugs! Robert is not the top priority because he has at least some level of experience with living in unstable environments and on the streets and is going to be virtually impossible to place, but I can find a place for Melinda if we can get that disability taken care of. This living situation is definitely worse than the homeless shelter but jumping in to take guardianship of her definitely breaks up her plan for her life, which is to be with her boyfriend and start a family. I don't know if it is a forever thing or not but compared to the rest of the experiences they have had, this romance is a pretty wonderful thing for them. It would be devastating to just grab her and say "you're coming with us" and take her an hour and a half out of town to some place where she will never even know how to contact Robert again. I don't want to leave anyone in a dangerous situation, but I also don't want to rob anyone of a chance at happiness.*

Sean stepped off the sagging porch steps and began walking down the driveway. As he stepped into the car, he looked back at the group of four that had gathered on the porch to see him off.

Robert had a huge smile, waving enthusiastically, with his other arm around Melinda's shoulders. Melinda looked down, maybe at the ground or at a stain on her nightgown. Nick had turned to go inside, and Jessie stared intently at Sean with her hand on her hip.

Melinda is a vulnerable adult here, Sean thought, *but anything I might do to protect her would separate her from Robert. I want to make sure she is safe, but I also want to respect that Melinda and Robert deserve to have a relationship. I sure don't want to be another part of the system just rolling over people. But this living situation makes me very uneasy. My supervisor will expect me to have a plan about how I would intervene or not so we can weigh the options, so I better think about what I need to do next.*

5 Involuntary Mindfulness

A cool breeze blew across the parking lot as Sharon Hart and fellow practicum student Nicole Stedman walked to Sharon's car. They had just finished co-leading their first trauma-focused mindfulness group at Washington Irving Elementary.

Sharon's eyes welled with tears as she broke the silence, "There is no way we are doing this again." She glanced at Nicole who nodded in agreement while wiping a tear from her cheek, adding "Something is going on here that is beyond our ability. We can't do this anymore. It just won't work."

Sharon glanced back at the imposing school building with metal grates over its windows that resembled those of a prison. *I have never seen kids so out of control*, Sharon thought, *not even when I was a school teacher. I know that they could be helped by group treatment, but the techniques simply didn't work. Worse yet, someone could have been hurt.*

Midtown Family Services

Midtown Family Services (MFS) had emerged as the largest provider of behavioral health care and family counseling in Marion County. The organization housed over 50 different programs that offered mental health counseling to adults and children, substance abuse treatment, and family focused services. Although the organization was most visibly recognized at their massive headquarters near downtown Indianapolis, the majority of their large staff was spread across dozens of offices throughout Marion County. They also employed a large number of community-based clinicians in school and home-based settings.

The organization had a Board of Directors, a CEO, and dozens of program and departmental supervisors. A nonprofit organization, MFS relied on a complex funding structure that included public funds, private donations, grants, insurance, and fee-for-service payments from clients. MFS also provided sliding scale services to uninsured families by assigning them to bachelor and graduate level practicum students and interns.

The Family Counseling Center

An MFS program, The Family Counseling Center (FCC) was located in East Indianapolis. FCC housed dozens of licensed clinicians, case managers, and practicum students that provided family-focused clinical services. Although FCC was an office-based clinical program, it was not uncommon for staff to interface and collaborate with other units throughout MFS.

Evelyn Faustine

The director of FCC was Evelyn Faustine, a licensed clinical social worker who had worked in multiple programs throughout MFS over the past 30 years. She was cheerful and positive with high energy and a bright smile. Although most of her staff would describe Evelyn as a supportive leader with a great deal of clinical wisdom, she was also known for her strength-based approach to supervision. New hires in the program would quickly learn that Evelyn had little interest in hearing about problems in their caseloads and would consistently refocus every conversation towards solutions. FCC had a robust practicum program and Evelyn served as the practicum instructor for a near constant rotation of graduate students. Her busy schedule made it impractical to meet one-on-one with her students aside from a weekly group supervision session. Because of this, Evelyn relied heavily on preceptors to oversee the work of her practicum students.

Danny Fernandez

Danny Fernandez had worked as a Licensed Professional Counselor (LPC) with MFS for seven years. Danny enjoyed his work at FCC and main-tained a large caseload in addition to duties as the lead preceptor for social work students and as field instructor for several undergraduate interns. Danny also led the weekly Therapy in Practice (TIP) meetings for FCC practicum students and had a reputation as an excellent teacher.

Sharon Hart

An MSW student in her early 40s, Sharon was a non-traditional student working on her third degree. After graduating with a bachelor's degree in theater, she applied to law school with the hope of pursuing her pas-sion for social justice as a civil rights attorney. After law school, she worked as an attorney for several years before quitting to be more available to her family. When her eldest child started pre-school, Sharon began a decade-long career as a pre-school and kindergarten teacher. As her kids grew older, she decided to return to her law practice and sought to become a certified mediator and collaborative divorce attorney, often working in high conflict divorce situations. The interdisciplinary nature of collaborative divorce practice exposed Sharon to a variety of mental health professionals, including social workers. She soon realized that her passion was more in line with the social work profession and she decided to pursue an MSW.

Nicole Stedman

Nicole was an MSW student in her early 20s who had become close friends with Sharon over the course of their studies at the Indiana University School of Social Work. Although she was young, she had been the director of a summer camp for several years and was very comfortable working with children and families.

Washington Irving School

Like most schools in Indianapolis, Washington Irving Elementary was struggling with the realities of state and local budget woes. The Indianapolis Public School district was experiencing a nearly $22 million deficit, but this didn't seem to damper principal Brooklyn Douglas's mood. Known to her students as "Mrs. B", Principal Douglas was energetic and a constant positive presence in the building. Like most other principals in the district, Principal Douglas needed to find ways to do more with less.

This was especially challenging given the demographics of her student population. Located in East Indianapolis, the surrounding neighborhood was infamous for having the highest homicide rate in Marion County. Over 70% of the students received free or reduced price lunches, and parental engagement was very low. The majority of the students identified as African American (55%), with 11% identifying as Latino and 26% as white.

Behavioral problems and other crises were very common at Washington Irving. Although the school was severely understaffed, the teachers and other school employees did their best to serve a student population that was often exposed to extreme environmental stressors in their homes and community. Principal Douglas leveraged many community resources to support her students. This included inviting MSF therapists to provide mental health and behavioral counseling in the building during school hours. She also relied heavily on a full-time school social worker to intervene and manage the daily flood of classroom and student emergencies.

An Invitation to Volunteer

In January of 2017, Sharon Hart and Nicole Stedman were two weeks into their concentration year practicum with FCC when Sharon received an email from her preceptor Danny:

Sent: 1/22/2017
To: Sharon Hart
From: Danny Fernandez
CC: Evelyn Faustine

Sharon,

Evelyn just told me about a grant MFS has received to implement a trauma-based mindfulness group at Washington Irving School. They would like to offer the group to students with behavioral problems who are at risk of suspension or expulsion. I think this would be a great opportunity for you and Nicole to incorporate into your practicum. Let me know what you think!

Regards,
Danny

This sounds like a huge project to take on so early in the practicum, Sharon thought, *but I know that Nicole is very interested in mindfulness practice and we both have lots of experience working with elementary school kids.* The request was certainly a departure from the planned activities that had been developed for the practicum placement, but it would only take a few hours per week to plan and facilitate the group. *Are we really in a position where we can decline?* Sharon thought as she imagined how such a conversation might go with Danny and Evelyn.

After a brief discussion, Nicole and Sharon decided to take on the mindfulness project. Danny scheduled a meeting with Principal Douglas to discuss goals for the group. He also suggested that they include Andrew, an undergraduate intern at FCC, in the project.

The Planning Meeting

"I'm actually attending a conference on mindfulness next month," Principal Douglas said excitedly as she welcomed Sharon, Nicole, and Andrew into her office, "I really hope this treatment will be effective with my students." The speed and intensity of her speech gave Sharon the impression that the meeting would be brief.

"How will you select which students will be in the group?" Nicole asked.

"Our school social worker will decide who gets to be in the group and she will pick them up from their classrooms and bring them to you." Principal Douglas responded.

She seems really busy, Sharon thought as Principal Douglas glanced at the clock for the third time in as many minutes. They spent the next few minutes discussing logistics like room size, number of participants, and timeframe.

"These kids have so much trauma in their lives," Principal Douglas continued, "most of them have witnessed violence in their families and in the community and many of them have parents who struggle with addiction."

Even though she had yet to meet the children, Sharon felt an intense sense of compassion for them. *It's horrible how these kids suffer in the community and are then misunderstood in school*, Sharon thought, *this should be a place where they can be supported and respected, not thrown into detention or expelled.*

"It sounds like there is a pretty wide age range of students you would like to include in our group," Sharon added, "Perhaps we could split your students into two groups?"

"I agree," Nicole jumped in, "we could do a 30 minute group with kids from kindergarten through second grade followed by a second 30 minute group with third grade through sixth."

"That sounds perfect. I'm really glad you're here and I think this group is going to be really helpful!" Principal Douglas said as she stood from her desk indicating that the meeting was over.

I'm not sure I have a clear vision of how this is going to work, Sharon thought as they left the principal's office. After voicing her concerns to Nicole and Andrew, they agreed to meet again in a few days to prepare for the first group session.

Sharon did some research on mindfulness practice with children prior to the next meeting with her co-facilitators. She shared her research at the planning meeting and they agreed to divide the group into beginning, middle, and end segments with each facilitator taking the lead at a different stage.

"My biggest concern is that we approach these kids in a manner that is respectful and therapeutic," Sharon said as she looked up from her notes, "I don't want to be another adult who talks to them in an angry or condescending manner."

"I agree," Nicole jumped in, adding, "I'm sure they get plenty of that from their teachers."

"Do you have any thoughts?" Sharon said as she made eye contact with Andrew who had been mostly silent during the meeting.

"Nope," Andrew responded, "sounds good to me."

Mindful Madness

The day of the first group, Sharon, Nicole, and Andrew carpooled to Washington Irving Elementary. "We are here for the mindfulness group," Sharon told the receptionist who didn't appear to be aware of the scheduled event.

"I'm sorry, Principal Douglas is in a meeting right now," the receptionist said as she glanced at her computer screen and clicked her mouse a few times. "Let me check with our social worker," she added picking up her phone.

"She's not answering." The receptionist tried a few more numbers to no avail. Sharon glanced at the clock, *we are supposed to start in 15 minutes! I was really hoping to have some time to set up the room and do some last minute preparations.*

A few more minutes passed as Sharon, Nicole, and Andrew anxiously made small talk with the school receptionist.

"There she is!" the receptionist exclaimed as she spotted the school social worker walking down the hall outside the front office.

"You must be here for the detention group," the social worker guessed as she entered the front office, "I'm still choosing which kids to send to your group, but I can take you to the room."

The room was clearly a multipurpose space. Some chairs had been set in a circle, shelves that extended up to the ceiling lined the walls, and several large room dividers segmented the space into three sections. The shelves were mostly empty with a few books and other items stored here and there. Nicole began stacking the chairs while Sharon placed carpet squares around the room for the kids to sit on. After a few minutes, they heard the echoes of children's voices down the hallway as the first group approached.

The once quiet and peaceful room erupted into a chaotic mixture of laughter and yelling with four or five separate conversations all occurring at the same time. *I thought we had decided to do the younger group first*, Sharon thought as ten children who were clearly older rushed into the room, shoving to get past each other. The school social worker appeared to be in a rush and she quickly left the room without a word after all the children had entered.

"We are going to get started now," Andrew said softly, his voice nearly inaudible above the rumble of the children. A few moments passed as Andrew stood silently at the front of the group. He made eye contact with Nicole, who responded to his non-verbal cry for help and immediately attempted to take control of the group.

"Okay, everyone! Let's get started. Who's heard the word mindfulness before?" Nicole's commanding voice captured the group's attention momentarily and she began to introduce the planned icebreaker. But her success was short-lived as the children returned to their previous, rambunctious state.

They clearly aren't buying what we are selling, Sharon thought as several kids began moving around the room, *no one has prepared them for this! They don't even know what mindfulness means. They just think they are in trouble and we are their detention babysitters.*

Seconds felt like minutes as the group facilitators exchanged nervous glances in the increasingly chaotic room. Several of the boys began to climb the shelving along the walls while another child began moving the room divider around. A few carpet squares flew through the air like frisbees and Sharon overheard several boys make sexualized comments about the girls. A boy removed his shirt and threw it across the room while yelling at another child. *Somebody is going to get hurt if we don't do something*, Sharon thought as she watched a boy climb a shelf until he was high enough to touch the ceiling. *Forget mindfulness! We need to do something to keep these kids from injuring themselves!* With both Nicole and Andrew having tried to intervene, Sharon stepped to the front of the room and channeled all the gravitas from her years as a school teacher to gain control of the room.

"Listen up! We are going to get started now!" she commanded. "Let's start by learning everyone's name."

As the group gradually settled down, Sharon gestured at a boy to give his name. "Hello everyone, my name is Princess Race Car!" the boy joked as the room erupted with laughter. Sharon attempted to ignore the behavior and moved on to the next child who also gave a fake name, as did the next and the one after that.

"If we can't be respectful, I am going to have to get the principal!" Sharon yelled as the room gradually slipped back into a state of chaos. Sharon's face became flushed as her frustration and anger increased.

Although the majority of the children had ignored her directive, Sharon noticed that two kids were actually sitting as requested and appeared willing to participate in the group. Andrew was standing in a corner of the room looking completely disoriented, like a deer in headlights. Sharon walked over to him and asked him to pull the two calm students aside and work with them independently. He seemed relieved to be told what to do.

While Andrew began working with the least problematic group members, Sharon redirected her attention to the rest of the group. *Perhaps something more kinesthetic could leverage the energy in this room*, Sharon thought as she suggested an alternate icebreaker that involved dancing and lots of movement. As Sharon and Nicole began to lead the activity there was glimmer of hope that they could still salvage the group, but it was short-lived. "Shake those big boobs!" shouted a boy as another joined in with an equally demeaning comment about Sharon's body. Although she attempted to ignore the behavior, it had already succeeded in derailing the effort to reengage with the group.

Out of the corner of her eye Sharon detected movement in the window to the hallway where ten kindergarten through second graders were lined up enjoying the show. *Is it already time for the next group?* Sharon thought as she let out a sigh of equal parts frustration and relief.

"If you will say your name, you can line up and go!" Nicole called out. The mayhem was amplified by the echoes of the hallway as the first group exited the room. The school social worker had been approaching with the younger group, but she turned on a dime and followed the scattering older kids, yelling, "Walk! Don't run!"

Without prompting, the younger children rushed into the room and began playing and giggling. *I really wish they hadn't witnessed that last group, but hopefully we can still turn this thing around*, Sharon thought as she straightened the carpet squares.

"Everybody find a carpet square and have a seat!" yelled Nicole as she glanced hopefully at Andrew to begin to facilitate the planned icebreaker. For several minutes it appeared as if the group would be able to function, but the children gradually began talking over the facilitators and moving around the room. Having witnessed the previous group playing on the shelving, several children began to climb while others began sliding underneath the room dividers. *One of these kids is going to fall and seriously injure themselves,* Sharon thought as a young boy managed to climb to the top shelf. *These kids will not listen to us! They are going to get hurt! We need to find a way to regain some semblance of authority and control here.*

Then Sharon remembered that they had brought puffed cheese balls to use as part of a mindful eating activity, *Maybe this would entice them to come back to the circle?* As she opened the bag of treats, several kids darted to the center of the room, knocking over one of the girls. While Sharon and Nicole tended to the girl they heard the door to the room open. *Thank goodness,* Sharon thought looking up hoping to see the school social worker or Principal Douglas, but there was no adult to be found. Instead, two of the boys had left the room and were running down the hallway at full speed.

"I'll go after them!" Nicole yelled as she ran out the door after the boys. Sharon stood in front of the door to make sure no other children would try to leave. She anxiously glanced out of the window into the hallway hoping to see Nicole and the two boys. *I don't even know their names! We'll need the school social worker to help us deduce who's missing from the group!*

Nearly 15 minutes passed before Nicole returned to the classroom without the boys.

"I can't find them anywhere," Nicole said, slightly out of breath.

"What if they left the building?" Sharon added with a slight panic in her voice.

Nicole left the room again, this time to find the school social worker or the principal. "I can't find anyone and the receptionist isn't at the front desk," Nicole said as she returned from this second effort empty handed.

Sharon turned back to the group of children who were still wildly moving around the room. *Someone is going to get hurt,* she fretted again.

"Everyone line up," Sharon commanded, "please go directly back to your homerooms." Sharon, Nicole, and Andrew stood silent for several moments as the children scattered down the hallway, hopefully returning to their classrooms. After a few moments, they started to gather their materials and straighten up the room.

As they walked to the front office, the hallway was eerily quiet. *Where are all the adults in the school?* Sharon thought as they approached the still empty front desk. They stood in the front office for a few moments before deciding to leave.

A cool breeze blew across the parking lot as Sharon, Nicole, and Andrew walked to the car. Sharon's eyes welled with tears as she broke the silence, "there is no way we are doing this again." She glanced at Nicole who nodded in agreement while wiping a tear from her cheek, adding "there's something going on here that is beyond our ability. We can't do this anymore. It just won't work."

Sharon glanced back at the imposing school building with metal grates over its windows that resembled those of a prison. *I have never seen kids so out of control,* Sharon thought, *not even when I was a school teacher. I know that they could be helped by group treatment, but the techniques simply didn't work. Worse yet, we don't even know if they all made it back to class safely. Someone could have been hurt.*

During the drive back to FCC the three continued to debrief the experience. "What if Evelyn doesn't let us quit?" Nicole worried. The thought of being forced to continue the grant for the remainder of her practicum sent a chill down Sharon's spine. *She likes to hear about solutions, not problems.*

6 Crossing the Borderline

Liv followed Penny, the leader of the *Survivors to Thrivers Group*, into her comfortable, clean office. Penny sat down at her tidy desk and clicked her mouse to open the template for group notes in the electronic medical record.

"Penny," Liv began, hesitantly. "Did you notice anything unusual about Rhonda today?"

"What do you mean?" Penny responded absently as she clicked through the template.

"I don't know, just the way she was sitting?" Liv responded. "Her gestures seemed different. Like she wasn't loud, wasn't animated, she just seemed off. What's your take on that?"

"You know she seemed fine to me," Penny said as she turned to look at Liv over her fashionable reading glasses. "I guess she was just having an off day."

"Yeah, maybe she is," Liv continued, "but I'm worried."

Boise, Idaho

With a population of about a quarter million, Boise was the largest city in the state of Idaho. It was considered a safe place to live, with a downtown that might not be as bustling as Seattle or Portland, but was pedestrian friendly and housed venues for theater and arts. The area around Boise State University was mostly residential, but had a college town feel within the city.

The population of Boise was 89% white, with the state of Idaho having a population that was 93% white. The state had seven geographical regions, all with community mental health centers administered by the state of Idaho Department of Health and Welfare, and Medicaid services branded as Optum Idaho. Various other nonprofits and mental health service centers operated throughout the city, but options were limited for clients without a method of payment.

The state of Idaho ranked at the very bottom of mental health funding per capita, in the company of Texas, Arkansas, Oklahoma, and Kentucky. Idaho was classified as a rural state, and had a significant shortage of mental health providers. Idaho was ranked last in the number of psychiatrists per person, despite high levels of mental illness in the population. It was the last state to develop and operate a suicide crisis hotline. The state legislature had made tremendous cuts in mental health funding in the recent years, and mental health facilities struggled to operate.

Boise Center for Mental Health

The Boise Center for Mental Health (BCMH) was a community mental health center that provided services for clients on Medicaid or Medicare, as well as clients without a pay source. BCMH offered a wide variety of mental health services including intake and assessment, medication management, case management, individual therapy, and group therapy. To stretch the limited funds and the ever-increasing numbers of clients, providers facilitated several groups a week with six to eight clients attending. The groups focused on issues like managing depression, overcoming anxiety, utilizing mindfulness skills, or relationship skills. They were usually led by a master's level therapist, but some of the more psychoeducational groups were led by bachelor's level providers. Individual therapy was also provided for high need clients, but was a limited resource.

Liv Fouassin

Olivia "Liv" Fouassin was a 29-year-old, white MSW student, working on her final practicum to complete her concentration in Direct Practice at Boise State University. She had earned her bachelor's degree in psychology in 2011 and worked as a psych technician for five years in an inpatient facility; first with adults with severe mental illnesses, and later with children with reactive attachment disorder.

Liv considered pursuing a master's in psychology, but inspired by the person-in-environment perspective, she "jumped ship" and began the MSW program in 2014, attending school part time and keeping her job at the inpatient facility. She moved in with her elderly grandmother, who needed care and came with conflict with Liv's oldest cousin. The cousin was an angry man with a history of domestic violence, and was listed as the closest relative for Liv's grandmother. While Liv was apprehensive about him, she felt generally able to handle the situation. He was rarely around and did little in the actual care of Liv's grandmother, and this living arrangement allowed her to support herself while in school.

When she began the MSW program, she had hoped to work in the field of substance abuse with veterans when she graduated. However, as the program introduced her to new ideas, she found that she enjoyed work in adult mental health. Her childhood had been difficult, with a mother who abused prescription opioids and a brother who had abused alcohol and had died by suicide as a young adult. She herself had attempted suicide years previously, reeling from the suffering of her family crises, and had undergone several years of therapy. Somewhere in the course of her own treatment, she had realized that her own struggles may be a strength that could inspire her to help others and she began to see some meaning in her own pain. She had a unique understanding of the painful lives of those who abused substances and suffered from mental illnesses, but also was keenly aware of the need to keep herself healthy and not assume her experiences were necessarily similar to her client's lives. She was proud of her recovery, and maintained a relationship with a therapist and psychiatrist to continue supporting her own mental health.

Survivors to Thrivers

The *Survivors to Thrivers Group* consisted of eight women, six of whom were diagnosed with Borderline Personality Disorder and all with extensive trauma histories. The women had all previously been in a variety of outpatient groups at the facility and were known for dominating the conversations, speaking aggressively to other members, and leading groups off topic. The mental health supervisor of the outpatient groups, LaTrice Germain, LMFT, a biracial woman in her 20s, had suggested a group be formed of just these women to implement some Dialectical Behavior Therapy (DBT) informed exercises and content.

"Perhaps if they are not with the other groups, those groups can be more successful," LaTrice had stated. "And the women would really benefit from the DBT related skills and a chance to practice their interpersonal communication with a group."

The women were not told this was the reason for the formation of the *Survivors to Thrivers Group*, as it was framed as an invitation only, closed group that would be capped at eight participants, and the women would all have a similar background of surviving trauma. The women found that appealing and were eager to join.

The group was led by Penny Faulkner, MSW, who was under supervision for her license as a clinical social worker. Penny was in her late 30s, bright, and small in stature. She dressed professionally in tailored suits, kept her blond hair in a well styled bob, and generally seemed calm, poised, and intelligent. Penny was also the individual therapist for some of the women in the group.

Tough Crowd

Liv entered the group room, set up with small desks and chairs in a U shape, and sat down at an open seat. The women filed into the room and looked expectantly at Penny, who was seated at a separate desk at the top of the U. Liv noticed that all of the women in the group were white, mostly in about their 30s or 40s.

One woman stood to the side of Liv and stared down at her. Liv became aware of her presence and looked up at the woman.

"Am I in your seat?" Liv asked. The woman nodded seriously.

"Oh, ok, sorry," Liv apologized sheepishly and moved two seats down to give the woman plenty of space. *Are these women glaring at me?* Liv wondered.

"Let's get started," Penny began. "This is Liv, an MSW student. She'll be sitting in on this group while she is here this semester, and co-facilitating as time goes by."

There was silence in the room. *No one is saying "hi" or "ok" or anything,* Liv thought. *Just crickets. I wish Penny had asked their permission or made sure it was ok with them. I guess I should do that.*

"Good morning," Liv began. "Is it ok with you ladies for me to sit in on this group? I know this is a closed group, but I would really love the chance to be a part of it."

Liv felt the heavy weight of the silence and the guarded stares of the women. Her thoughts were flying and her anxiety built as silence continued. *It's like they are thinking "who the fuck is the person, charging into our closed group, which you said would stay closed, and now there is this person, this STUDENT, who will just be here a little while."*

"Well, yeah, it is a closed group," stated one woman after the long silence. "But I guess I'm ok with trying it."

No one else spoke or even nodded, but Liv stayed and observed mostly in silence.

Rhonda From Brooklyn

The second group Liv attended included an exercise where Penny asked the women to close their eyes and listen to their surroundings, speaking aloud the sounds they could hear.

"I hear the leaves rustling outside," mentioned a member named Alison. "They sound dry and crinkling."

"I just heard a click when the heating system came on," said another member, Donna.

"I can hear people in the lobby, muffled voices," offered Rhonda. While the other women seemed to be relaxing, Rhonda was shifting in her chair, fidgeting with her pen, and crossing and uncrossing her legs. Her hair was long and unkempt, with bleached streaks and dark roots. She had numerous colorful tattoos on her arms.

After the exercise finished, Penny announced that they would now talk about distress tolerance a little before the session ended.

"All right!" Rhonda said loudly with a big, full laugh. "That mindful stuff is good, but I'm from Brooklyn and we just don't sit and say 'ommmmm' like that!"

"I don't think you need to make fun of it," Alison retorted. "Penny is trying to teach us some important stuff here." Alison was thin, dressed in a white shirt, with a neat blond ponytail.

"Naw," Rhonda responded. "Not making fun, just having fun. No need to get on to me, I'm trying too."

I was warned this group could argue and get pretty heated, Liv thought. *But it seems these women speak their minds and are learning to resolve conflicts.*

"Different strokes for different folks," Rhonda added. Alison nodded.

"Ladies," Penny began, "Let's move on to the distress tolerance portion of the group today. How could you describe your schema that leads you to overreact to distress and engage in self sabotaging behaviors?"

Again, Liv did not offer additional intervention in the group, but did make a few statements to reflect and clarify with the members. Still focusing on building rapport, she thanked the group for letting her attend again.

Jumping In

The next week, Penny picked back up on the theme of distress tolerance, and repeated her question she stated in the group with the previous week.

"How could you describe your schema that leads you to overreact to distress and engage in self sabotaging behaviors?" Penny asked, looking down at her notes.

Liv remembered there had been little reaction to this question last time. She looked around the room and noticed blank looks. *Penny seems so smart, she really knows her shit,* Liv thought. *I'm not sure the women know words like "schema" though. I wouldn't if I didn't have psychology and social work degrees!*

"How would you classify your cognitive schema?" Penny rephrased.

"Does everyone know what a schema is?" Liv asked hesitantly. She glanced over at Penny, hoping she had not overstepped.

"I have no idea," said Emily, sitting on the side of the room with Alison and Donna.

"No fucking clue," chimed in Rhonda. She laughed and gestured her hands widely with an exaggerated shrug.

Liv glanced at Penny again, who was looking down at her notes. *Is she surprised? Or offended?* Liv thought. *Oh well, I've started this and need to finish it.*

"Well, a schema is kind of like a pattern," Liv explained. "A pattern of how you think, like a framework of the way you take in information and interpret it. So let's say a child had a schema that it didn't matter how hard she studied, she could never do well in school because she was just not smart. That would really affect how she interpreted everything that happened at school, right?"

"Sure," agreed Marti, sitting to the right of Rhonda. "Every time she did bad, it would be more proof she was dumb. School was always like that for me, just more and more people telling me I couldn't do things right."

"Right, so what would that lead her to do next, if that was her schema?" Liv followed up.

"Just say 'fuck it'," Rhonda offered. "I can't do it, so why even give a shit?"

Liv smiled. *You can always depend on Rhonda to say something colorful,* she thought.

"So what words can you use to describe your schema?" Penny interjected. The women offered many ideas, seeming now to understand the question. As the group wrapped up, she heard Marti and Rhonda talking as they left.

"Rhonda, don't you have your biopsy and all coming up soon?" Marti had asked her.

"Yeah," Rhonda replied. "We'll see what the docs want to do to me!" She said casually.

Later, Liv asked Penny if she knew more about Rhonda's health.

"Yes," Penny had answered, "she has breast cancer. They found the lump and they did some more tests and said it was cancerous, but I think this next appointment is to figure out how advanced it is and what the treatment plan may be."

"I had no idea," Liv responded. *Rhonda seemed so boisterous, kind of cantankerous and ornery in the group. She didn't seem to have the affect I'd expect of someone dealing with a breast cancer diagnosis.*

Taking the Reins

"Liv," said LaTrice, "I just got a call from Penny and she's not feeling well today. Do you think you could run the *Survivors to Thrivers Group* this afternoon?"

"OK, I'll do my best," Liv answered, swallowing hard.

When it was time for group, Liv was surprised to see that Penny had come in just for the group and was sitting in her usual spot.

"Liv, I came in just so you don't feel abandoned," Penny said weakly, "but I don't feel well at all. How about if you facilitate the group today and I'll help out if you are stuck. Is that ok?"

"Sure," Liv answered. "Thank you for coming in, and I hope you feel better."

The women filed into the group room, and Liv immediately noticed Rhonda. Today, Rhonda didn't have a wild frizz of unkempt hair or a bright tank top that showed off her tattoos. She wore a large sweatshirt with the hood up, and she quietly took her seat. She set her hands flat on the table, with her fingers fanned out, and looked down at them, stoically.

"Rhonda," Liv began gently, "I wonder if you'd like to start off our check in today. What are you hoping to accomplish in group today?"

"I went to the doctor this morning," Rhonda stated flatly. "They say this cancer's terminal, stage four, and there's nothing they can do about it."

The room was silent, until Donna spoke.

"Rhonda, don't give up," Donna said, "Those doctors don't know everything."

Rhonda nodded slightly. "There is rhyme and reason to the world," she said.

The other women murmured platitudes, about being sorry to hear the news and offers to help, but Rhonda nodded again, stating, "it is what it is."

"And yeah, no kidding the doctors don't know everything," chimed in Marti. "Like just look how long it is taking for my doctors to do what they need to do to help me get disability."

"You know, why are you trying to get disability?" Alison responded. "You are perfectly capable of getting up off your ass and working. We've all been through plenty of abuse, I was in an abusive marriage too, and most of us are not too lazy to work."

"My diagnosis prevents me from working," Marti responded, "I can't hold down a job."

"Maybe your diagnosis is 'lazy ass'," Alison replied sarcastically.

Here we go with the conflict and putting out fires, Liv thought. *I don't want to take a side, but I need to try to steer this back to something therapeutic and not just fighting.*

"It's hard to work sometimes, but I do it," Donna chimed in. "You just suck it up and do it."

"But it is really nobody's place to judge someone else's progression and what they've been through with their diagnosis," Liv interjected, playing peacemaker. "Alison, you don't know what Marti has been through completely and Marti doesn't know what you've been through either."

"We've all been through a lot, like Alison said though," said Emily. "We've all had to work and raise kids even if we struggle with trauma or drinking or whatever else."

"Yeah, but drinking, that's different," Donna added. "I don't think anyone should get disability because they're a drunk."

"But I'm terminal," Rhonda said softly. "And I know I'm a recovering alcoholic and haven't had a drink in 19 years, but if I'm terminal I might as well enjoy myself."

"But that's not why you get disability!" Donna continued. "Not for drinking, but for other conditions that weren't your fault!"

"I don't think it is fair to say that drinking is someone's fault," Emily said quietly. "I mean, maybe, but it is still really hard to get through."

"You just need to let go," Rhonda said.

"That's what they say in Al-Anon," Emily responded. The group launched a lively discussion of their experiences with 12 Step Groups and wildly divergent views of effectiveness.

I want to say something to follow up with Rhonda, Liv thought, *as I feel like she needs to talk. But I can't get a word in with all these little arguments being thrown at me to referee.*

As the group ended, Liv tried to get Rhonda's attention to ask her to stay, but Rhonda kept her eyes down and quickly left the group room.

Something Seems Off

Liv followed Penny, the leader of the *Survivors to Thrivers Group*, into her comfortable, clean office. Penny sat down at her tidy desk and clicked her mouse to open the template for group notes in the electronic medical record.

"Penny," Liv began, hesitantly. "Did you notice anything unusual about Rhonda today?"

"What do you mean?" Penny responded absently as she clicked through the template.

"I don't know, just the way she was sitting?" Liv responded. "Her gestures seemed different. Like she wasn't loud, wasn't animated, she just seemed off. What's your take on that?"

"You know she seemed fine to me," Penny said as she turned to look at Liv over her fashionable reading glasses. "I guess she was just having an off day."

"Yeah, maybe she is," Liv continued, "But I'm worried."

"Liv," Penny said kindly. "Why are you worried? Group went great. It was your first time leading the group, and you did an awesome job. I am really impressed with you."

"Thank you for that," Liv responded, "But I feel like something else is there."

"What do you mean?" Penny asked, turning back to face the computer screen.

"Well, she has an extensive trauma history, she has three previous suicide attempts, and she just got a terminal diagnosis like today," Liv offered with increasing urgency. "And she was making those comments that just seemed so ... existential."

"That could just be her way of coping," Penny responded. "Honestly though, I didn't see a problem. I thought she just seemed relaxed and comfortable."

Why would anyone be relaxed after hearing about a terminal illness? Liv thought.

"Do you mind if we follow up with that?" Liv asked. "Maybe we could give her a call just to check on her?"

"No, we have to do this group note and you know they take forever," Penny answered. "I don't really have time to make a phone call because I have a client in 15 minutes. So no, calling is not the right thing to do for this client. She has a session scheduled and can talk with the group. Here you go, the note is ready for you to write in your observations and interventions for each member now. We better get started."

Liv sat down in Penny's chair as Penny rose and stepped aside to watch Liv document the session. But as she typed, Liv just could not shake the feeling in her gut that something just was not right with Rhonda. *Penny is probably just thinking I'm hypersensitive. She is smart and she knows this client, and I'm just new here. And she's probably right, I know I am self-conscious about reading too much into things just because I've been through them. Maybe I'm relating too much and putting myself in the equation. But what if I'm not?*

7 Don't Speak Too Much

"I just met with the finance department and I need to know why Guadalupe Fernandez is still here. She is illegal and you know we won't be able to find a dialysis placement for her," Katy's soft yet firm voice sounded fuzzy coming from the speakerphone. Monica sighed in frustration as she made eye contact with her field instructor, Linda Kawar.

"She's not undocumented," Linda patiently reminded Katy, "she is a legal resident and we are trying to get her on Medicare so she can receive outpatient dialysis. Her husband is a citizen and has paid Medicare taxes for over 40 work quarters."

"Next time make sure Monica places a sticky note on their chart so we know their ... you know ... legality," Katy paused briefly, then continued "to know if the patient is documented or undocumented. Regardless, she is medically stable right now and we need to discharge her." Katy's tone was decisive as she ended the call.

"She's just going to end up back in the hospital in a week! Or worse—she might die!" Monica's plea was louder than she intended and Linda's expression hardened.

"I know you feel bad about this situation, but there is nothing we can do." Linda clearly did not want to discuss the matter further, and the finality of her words echoed in Monica's mind as she walked back to her office.

I bet I would have a sticky note on my file if I was a patient at this hospital. We never discharge patients with end-stage renal disease until there are arrangements in place for outpatient dialysis. I doubt anyone with white skin would be subjected to this kind of treatment. How can I get this client the care she needs if everyone in this system seems bent on discharging her regardless of how this will impact her health?

Second Generation Latinx

Monica was the second oldest of five children who lived with their parents in *El Pueblo* neighborhood in Wichita, Kansas. Although their neighborhood was currently a thriving district of Latinx owned businesses, Monica and her family had been the only bilingual family on their street when she was in elementary school. Monica was born and raised in Wichita after her parents immigrated from a small village in Mexico in the mid-1980s. The couple obtained legal resident status and Monica's father eventually became a naturalized citizen.

Despite having lived in Wichita for 30 years and having had five U.S.-born children, Monica's mother had not felt confident in her English language skills and was intimidated by the citizenship process. Her father was a textbook case of immigrant bootstrapping and had been able to save enough money as a construction worker over the years to buy several rental properties in Wichita. His landlord income allowed him to retire from his construction work and enabled him to fully fund the college education of all five of his children.

Monica was only the second person in her family with a bachelor's degree. Living in her older sister's shadow, it was never a question that she would go to college and major in business. About a year into her degree it became clear that business was not a good fit for her passion and personality. "I just want to help people!" she would tell her parents who were equal parts support and stress in her college pursuits. As she discussed her frustration with peers, she was introduced to a social work faculty member in the Wichita State University School of Social Work. This connection evolved into a mentorship as Monica changed her major to Social Work. After graduating with her BSW, she was accepted to Wichita State's MSW program. Soon, her siblings would be living under Monica's shadow as she was to be the first member of her family to earn a master's degree.

Via Christi Hospital

Throughout her social work education, Monica had been particularly interested in medical social work. She had first-hand experience translating for her mom in doctor's appointments and was always bothered by the way in which non-English speaking patients were treated. As a medical social worker, she hoped to be an advocate for the Latinx community. In her final year of the MSW program, Monica was thrilled to be accepted as a practicum student at Via Christi Hospital. The social work practicum was embedded in the Clinical Care Management department at the hospital.

Monica's interview for the practicum was conducted by Katy Anastas, the social work supervisor in Clinical Care Management. An LCSW, Katy was the direct supervisor of the case management and social work teams at Via Christi. Most of the case managers were registered nurses and their work primarily focused on assisting patients in obtaining medical equipment. The social workers had more broadly defined roles that included in-depth assessment, brief solution-focused interventions, and referrals to outpatient services. The interview went very well and Katy, in her typical soft-spoken manner, was enthusiastic about Monica's Spanish language skills and passion for medical social work.

Monica's field instructor was Linda Kawar, one of the floor social workers. Like Katy, Linda was soft-spoken and had a calming presence. Also an LCSW, she had a strong accent that Monica couldn't quite place, but guessed might be from Iran or Iraq.

Over the first few months of practicum, Monica quickly adapted to the demands of social work in the hospital. In particular, Monica came to understand that an informal role for social workers was to serve as "creative" discharge planners. This was especially clear during the weekly department meetings that primarily focused on discussing the status of patients that had been in the hospital for more than five days. The pressure to justify continued admission of patients who did not have clear medical orders was intense and occasionally combative during the staff meetings. In fact, Monica noticed a sense of urgency on Linda's part to discharge as many patients as possible prior to the weekly meeting.

"The last thing we want is to draw attention to ourselves," Linda would often say to the social work staff. "Don't speak too much," was a common refrain, "just keep your head down and try to solve problems, not cause them." Monica was very much aware of the political realities and the pressures placed on Katy and Linda. The financial department was in regular contact with the Clinical Care Management team and there was a clear norm of "be seen and not heard" when Monica was rotating with different doctors.

Soy Residente

As Monica arrived at Via Christi on a Monday morning in late March, she was pleased to see that she would be rotating with Dr. Bengali. Of all the physicians she had worked with, Dr. Bengali was one of the only doctors who would regularly include the social workers and nurses in his conversation with patients. People were always surprised when the tall, silver haired, white man revealed his strong accent. Monica never had the opportunity to ask, but it sounded like a stereotypical Middle-Eastern accent. As Monica looked over the patient list for the morning, she recognized several Latinx sounding names. It had become an informal policy to "group" Spanish speaking clients and assign them to the physician that Monica was scheduled to rotate with. One benefit was that Monica could facilitate communication between the doctor and the patient if needed and she also would likely be asked to take the lead with Spanish speaking families anyway. Most non-English speaking patients had family members or friends available to translate, so Monica was only rarely asked to assist with translating for doctors and other staff.

As Dr. Bengali worked through his patient rotations, Monica noticed that their next patient was named Guadalupe Fernandez. Monica was mindful to never make assumptions about a patient's linguistic abilities, but still wondered if she might need to help with communication with this patient. As Monica entered the room, she was struck by how Guadalupe looked much older than 54, the listed age on her medical chart. She had short grey hair and her skin was wrinkly with slight bruising on her arms. Standing next to her was her husband Francisco, who looked younger than Guadalupe despite the fact that he was nearly 15 years her elder. Guadalupe appeared to be a little overweight, but this may have been due to fluid buildup from poorly managed kidney disease. "Your blood pressure is dangerously high and you absolutely must do more to manage your diabetes," Dr. Bengali said as he flipped through Guadalupe's chart. Francisco was sitting on the other side of the bed and leaned forward to translate the doctor's statement.

"You're going to need dialysis three times weekly if you want to live," Dr. Bengali continued in his typical no-nonsense manner. Guadalupe smiled and nodded gently as the doctor spoke.

"No mas dime lo que tengo que hacer. Yo hago lo que usted diga," she responded after her husband translated the doctor's statements.

"Your kidneys aren't functioning like they should, and dialysis will really help with the fluid buildup you've been experiencing," Dr. Bengali leaned forward slightly to emphasize the importance of his statements, "you will need dialysis at least three times a week."

Guadalupe's affect shifted slightly as her husband translated the doctor's words. Dr. Bengali continued to speak as he wrote on his clipboard, "You will need to stay here for at least another day or two until you are medically stable."

After Dr. Bengali left the room, Monica stayed behind to finish her assessment with the family. She learned that Francisco had moved to Wichita several decades earlier for work and had been a naturalized citizen for ten years. Francisco and Guadalupe were months away from celebrating their 35th wedding anniversary. They had ten children and 15 grandchildren, most of whom lived in Mexico. Only two of their adult children, Eduardo and Mariana, lived in Wichita.

"¿Cual es el estatus migratorio de usted?" Monica never felt comfortable asking questions about immigration status, but she knew that the answer would profoundly impact the kinds of services that might be available. "La razon de que yo pregunto es porque esto afecta las opciones que tenemos para ayudarla," Monica continued.

"Soy residente," Guadalupe responded, "tengo diez anos de residencia." Monica was visibly relieved to hear of Guadalupe's legal residency status. *This should make it easier to find funding for outpatient dialysis*, she thought as she finished up her assessment.

Me Dijeron Que No

Monica continued to visit with Guadaulpe and her family periodically over the next few days. There was always a family member in the room with Guadalupe, but Francisco was only able to come in the evenings due to his work schedule. Usually Mariana or Eduardo's wife, Flor, were in the room. Monica knew that her time with the family was limited and that there would be a lot of pressure to discharge Guadalupe as soon as she was medically stable. Almost all patients with end-stage renal disease needed to apply for Medicare benefits to cover the enormous costs of dialysis treatments.

"We can accept her as long as she has Medicare," the receptionist at Health Innovations Dialysis confirmed. Monica had anticipated this response and began dialing the extension to the hospital financial counseling department to make a referral.

"Hi, I need to refer Guadalupe Fernandez to start a Medicare application," Monica began before Nick, a patient advocate, interrupted. "We've already looked at this case and there is nothing we can do at this time. She's not a citizen and she doesn't have enough work quarters to qualify for Medicare."

Monica was caught off guard by this response and took a few moments to collect her thoughts before responding, "She is a legal resident and has some work hours and her husband is a U.S. citizen. If she doesn't qualify under her own work record, she will certainly qualify under her husband's. He has paid Medicare taxes for over ten years."

"This patient does not qualify for Medicare and we will not be wasting any time on an application. We can't have illegals using up all the resources that should go to real Americans," Nick responded tersely.

No human being is illegal! Monica thought as she gritted her teeth. A few awkward moments of silence followed as Monica regained her composure and continued, "Like I said, she is a legal resident and I've seen people in similar situations qualify for assistance in the past."

"This is a job that I do all day, every day, and I'm telling you that she will not qualify." Nick didn't hide his disdain and irritation at Monica's insistence and ended the call before she could reply.

Monica was no stranger to the type of language and argument she had just witnessed, but she was not expecting to encounter this type of thinking in a professional hospital setting. *Maybe he's just being lazy*, Monica mused. It certainly would be more complicated than a typical Medicare application, but Monica was confident that Guadalupe would qualify like most patients with end-stage renal disease.

Still fuming from her conversation with Nick, Monica marched down to Guadalupe's room. *This makes no sense! If we can't get her on Medicare, she will have to use the hospital as her primary source of dialysis treatment. It's a huge waste of resources and it will put a huge financial strain on this family. If I don't help them with this application, no one will.* As she entered the room, Monica sat next to Guadalupe and told her that they would need to initiate the Medicare application on their own. She wrote the number to the regional Medicare office on a sheet of paper and handed it to Guadalupe.

"You need to call this number to start the application process. I know that you qualify and I'll be back to check on you in a few hours."

Monica walked back to her office hoping to debrief with Kay or Linda, but neither was immediately available. *Surely this type of treatment won't be sanctioned by hospital administration.* Monica considered telling Dr. Bengali about her interaction with Nick. Before she gave in to the temptation, she remembered Linda's motto, *Try to solve problems, not cause them.*

"Me dijeron que no puedo hacer la aplicación," Guadalupe told Monica that afternoon when she came back to check on their progress. *I know they qualify! They must have explained their situation poorly*, Monica thought as she pulled a chair up to the phone next to Guadalupe's bed.

"Sé que calificas," Monica reassured her as she dialed the number to the regional Medicare office. After nearly an hour of speaking to several individuals at the Medicare office, including nearly 30 minutes on hold, Monica was finally able to secure an appointment for the family to initiate the Medicare application.

"Aqui esta el papel con toda la informacion de la cita para la aplicacion de Medicare. Es muy importante que vayan porque ellos son los que van a pagar por el tratamiento de dialysis." Monica was confident that Guadalupe would qualify, but the appointment with the Social Security Administration office was nearly a month away. *I need to find a clinic that will accept her based on anticipated Medicare coverage.*

Monica had still not been able to speak to Linda or Katy the following day before rounds with Dr. Bengali. "Overall, you seem to have stabilized and should be fine to leave the hospital as long as you continue to receive dialysis moving forward," he said while skimming Guadalupe's chart. The mention of discharge caught Monica off guard. *I'm not sure any of the outpatient dialysis clinics will take her without Medicare. I need more time to make arrangements before discharge.*

"I'm sorry doctor, but might it be possible to keep her here a little longer? I'm trying to find an outpatient dialysis clinic, but the process has been complicated by her status as a legal resident. She doesn't have enough work quarters, but her husband does." Monica rarely spoke during rounds, and it was a nerve-racking experience to confront Dr. Bengali in such a direct manner.

After a few moments of awkward silence, Dr. Bengali responded, "Of course! Just tell me when you have a placement and I will discharge her. We really need to do more as a country to fix this broken immigration system so people can get the resources they need!"

Monica had witnessed Dr. Bengali's semi-political rants before. He continued to ramble for several minutes, sometimes in a nearly inaudible mumble as he glanced out the window or at a daytime talk show on the muted television. Neither Monica or Flor attempted to translate the rant aside from telling Guadalupe that the doctor was going to keep her in the hospital until they could find an outpatient dialysis placement.

Don't Speak Too Much

Monica knew that her efforts to buy more time for Guadalupe would certainly be challenged at the weekly staff meeting. *I need to run this by Linda as soon as possible.* As she sat in the chair across from Linda's desk and explained Guadalupe's situation, Monica could practically read Linda's mind as her face reflected her discomfort.

"As you are aware, the hospital has a new director and I really think it's a bad idea to insist on keeping Guadalupe inpatient." Linda's voice was firm. "The last thing we want to do is to draw attention to the social work department." Monica felt irritated by Linda's sentiments, but her response was interrupted by a ringing landline. The call was from Katy and Linda answered it on speakerphone.

"I just met with the finance department and I need to know why Guadalupe Fernandez is still here. She is illegal and you know we won't be able to find a dialysis placement for her," Katy's soft yet firm voice sounded fuzzy coming from the speakerphone. Monica sighed in frustration as she made eye contact with Linda.

"She's not undocumented," Linda patiently reminded Katy, "she is a legal resident and we are trying to get her on Medicare so she can receive outpatient dialysis. Her husband is a citizen and has paid Medicare taxes for over 40 work quarters."

"Next time make sure Monica places a sticky note on their chart so we know their … you know … legality," Katy paused briefly, then continued "to know if the patient is documented or undocumented. Regardless, she is medically stable right now and we need to discharge her." Katy's tone was decisive as she ended the call.

"She's just going to end up back in the hospital in a week! Or worse—she might die!" Monica's plea was louder than she intended and Linda's expression hardened.

"I know you feel bad about this situation, but there is nothing we can do." Linda clearly did not want to discuss the matter further, and the finality of her words echoed in Monica's mind as she walked back to her office.

I bet I would have a sticky note on my file if I was a patient at this hospital. We never discharge patients with end-stage renal disease until there are arrangements in place for outpatient dialysis. I doubt anyone with white skin would be subjected to this kind of treatment. How can I get this patient the care she needs if everyone in this system seems bent on discharging her regardless of how this will impact her health?

With only a month left in her practicum, Monica wondered what the consequences might be should she attempt to advocate for Guadalupe with Dr. Bengali again. *He's the only other person in the hospital who has shown compassion for this family and he's not scared of administration like Katy and Linda. If I'm insubordinate, they might terminate my practicum and I would have to start over. But I have an ethical duty to advocate for my clients—how am I any different from the rest of this department if I abandon my principles to protect my practicum placement? Do I even want to work in this field anymore?*

Part III
New MSW Graduates

8   A Day in the Life

Although still in her first year of post-MSW practice and clinical supervision for licensure, Laura Burns was very comfortable in her role as a Child Welfare Specialist. When she went to see her agency supervisor, Mary Knowles, it was because she had reached an impasse and needed advice. Laura was stressed out when she entered Mary's office and sat down in the stiff wooden chair, leaning forward with her elbows on her knees and her face in her hands. She had always disliked the chair in Mary's office; it made her feel very uncomfortable. However, uncomfortable was exactly how she felt right now, and in this moment she found it oddly consoling. Mary sat looking out the window.

"This is a very difficult situation and one you must handle carefully," Mary intoned.

"Exactly. I just don't know what to do," Laura replied. "But I think Brenda's girls might be at risk for abuse."

"Would it be okay if we talked about this tomorrow? I have a meeting in two minutes," Mary said. "Maybe you can talk about this in your clinical supervision session?"

Laura sat for a moment before getting up and walking out of the office. She wondered if a true resolution could really be found. She was looking forward to asking advice from her clinical supervisor, too.

Laura Burns and the Agency

The Department of Family and Protective Services (DFPS) had about 250 offices located throughout the state of Texas and all had the same mission: "Protect children, the elderly, and people with disabilities from abuse, neglect, and exploitation by involving clients, families and communities" (www.dfps. state.tx.us). A total of four divisions made up DFPS, including child protective services, adult protective services, child care licensing, and prevention and early intervention.

Laura had been working in the Child Protective Services division of the DFPS in Abilene, Texas for one year. She initially moved to Abilene not just because there was an actual job opportunity with DFPS, but also because it seemed like a good place to raise a family. A population of about 115,000 held the promise of a small town feel with just enough big city advantages. Laura grew up in Austin, Texas and decided to go local when she went to the

University of Texas for both her bachelor's and her master's. After getting her bachelor's in psychology, she decided to get her MSW, in part because she liked the employment flexibility the degree offered. It took some time to find the right job in the right place, but Laura believed she had found it working for DFPS in Abilene.

Working for DFPS could at times be quite stressful; however, Laura found it to be very rewarding. Her numerous duties included visiting families' homes, educating families about behaviors that might lead to child abuse/neglect, and even removing children from homes that seemed unsafe. Despite all her different duties she always made sure that the children came first, knowing that their safety was of the utmost importance.

Thus far, Mary had helped her extensively in any problems she had on the job. Laura always felt that Mary had a good perspective on a wide range of situations. Laura was also working to become a Licensed Clinical Social Worker (LCSW) and thus was receiving clinical supervision outside DFPS. John Wagner had proven to be very resourceful, and Laura knew that she could count on John to provide direction in case she ran into a particularly troublesome situation. It was nice having two different people with whom to consult.

Brenda Schneider

It was 12:00 noon and Laura was getting ready to make her first home visit of the day. She pulled into a parking space at the Meadowland apartment building. At least she thought it was a parking space. It was hard to tell because the dividing lines had long since faded away. This was consistent with the aesthetic of the buildings, as they were in desperate need of a paint job. Stepping out of her car, Laura had to avoid an old hamburger wrapper and some ketchup, but she made it safely to the sidewalk and started towards the apartment.

She was going to visit Brenda Schneider, who had just been reunited with the last of her four children. Laura was proud of Brenda, and was looking forward to the visit. When Brenda opened the door, Laura could tell that Brenda was feeling better, perhaps better than she had felt in a long time. After all this time, she had finally regained custody of her children and seemed to be standing on her own two feet. Section 8 housing wasn't ideal for her and her four kids, but Brenda had worked hard to get her children back and standing there with them, Laura knew it was worth it. Brenda immediately began recounting to her how excited she was the day she found out the children were coming home.

"I was talking with my neighbor, James, sharing with him how excited I was to have them back," Brenda recalled. "He seemed really happy for me, and even offered to watch them if I ever got into a bind at work."

"I don't think I have met James. Is he the guy that lives across the breezeway?" Laura asked.

"That's him. He really is nice, but I think he kind of has a crush on me, although I am not interested in him in that way."

Laura was relieved. Although she didn't know this guy James, she really wanted Brenda to be careful with whom she associated, much less dated. Her last relationship ended when her boyfriend beat her oldest child who was five years old, putting him in the hospital. After he left, Brenda couldn't support herself and ended up homeless for a while. That was when the kids were taken into protective custody. Laura didn't want anything to mess up what had taken Brenda months to accomplish.

Laura and Brenda went over the treatment plan, making sure that the goals they had set were being met, and considering what needed to be done in the future. Laura also got a chance to spend some time around the children, who all seemed happy to be living at home with their mother again. Laura looked at her watch and stood up.

"I'm sorry Brenda, I have another appointment and need to run. But I'm glad you're doing okay. I'll be back in the next few weeks to see how everything is going. In the meantime, if you need anything, just give me a call."

"I will," Brenda responded. "Thanks again."

"No problem."

As Laura was leaving the building, she happened to run into the apartment manager, Lisa Mathers. Although they had only spoken briefly in the past, Lisa knew that Laura had clients in the apartment, including Brenda. Laura was in a hurry, but Lisa seemed determined to talk, so Laura stopped for a minute, while also keeping an eye on her watch.

"How can I help you?" Laura asked.

"I'm a little bit concerned about Brenda. That is, I'm concerned about her neighbor, James."

This took Laura by surprise, as she had just talked about James with Brenda.

"What do you mean?" Laura asked.

"Well, it's just that James's wife died a couple of years ago, and I don't want him getting taken advantage of, you know. He already has enough to deal with being a single parent and all, and he's just nice enough to get involved with someone who would use him," Lisa explained. "Frankly, he doesn't need to get hooked up with her."

"Thanks for the information. I'll keep my eyes open," Laura said as she hurried to the car.

Meredith Greene

Laura was in a hurry because one of her other clients was being reunified with her daughter at 2 P.M., and Laura promised her that she would be there when it happened. As she was pulling up to the DFPS building she saw Meredith Greene, who looked both anxious and excited. Just six weeks ago she was reunified with her 6-year-old daughter, Stephanie, and now she was finally being reunited with her 14-year-old daughter, Stacy. Laura got out of the car and walked up to Meredith.

"How are you holding up?" Laura asked.

"I'm so nervous I can barely keep still," Meredith responded.

"I certainly understand that," Laura said.

Laura had no doubt that Meredith was nervous. Her relationship with Stacy had always been awkward, in part because after Stephanie was born, Meredith focused most of her energy on the baby, ignoring Stacy. But Laura had been working to repair that relationship, and things had been better lately. Laura looked over at Stephanie, and when Stephanie looked up at her, Laura smiled. Stephanie did not return the smile. Meredith wasn't the only one nervous about the reunification. Laura knew Meredith and Stacy had a fragile relationship, and it was going to be a long road to repairing it.

While they were waiting, Laura asked, "Is there anything you need?"

"Not really. I've been doing pretty good, getting ready for Stacy's return, working, the usual. My neighbor James has also been pretty helpful, we went to the store together to get groceries."

Laura should've seen this coming, in part because Meredith lived on the first floor, directly below Brenda in the apartment complex. Originally Meredith lived on the other side of the complex, but her ex-husband, Thomas Cauldwell, moved into a building across the street that faced Meredith's apartment. In this way, he was able to keep tabs on her as she came and went. It was because of this that Meredith got a protective order against him and moved to the other side of the complex into a different apartment. Meredith didn't want Thomas anywhere near her daughters. Their divorce came on the heels of the discovery that he was sexually abusing Stacy, Meredith's daughter from another marriage. After it was found out, Stacy was placed into therapeutic foster care. Although Laura got the impression that Meredith felt bad not letting him see Stephanie, the child they had together, she was glad Meredith decided to get the protective order against him.

"Here she comes," Laura said, noting that Stacy had just walked out the doors.

Meredith took a few steps forward as Stacy approached her. Both seemed tentative. It was Stacy who broke the silence.

"Hi, mom."

"Hi, sweetheart," Meredith responded.

"Hey, Laura," Stacy said.

"Hi, Stacy. Feeling okay?" Laura asked.

"Yeah, I'm just glad I'm going home."

Laura spent a few more moments talking to Stacy and Meredith, but didn't want to keep them too long, as Stacy seemed ready to leave and Stephanie had become bored ten minutes ago.

"Ready to go home?" Meredith asked.

"Yeah. Let's go."

Laura watched them walk to the car, get in, and drive away. All things considered, it had gone well, but only time would tell exactly how things would turn out. Laura looked at her watch, realizing she hadn't eaten lunch, and that she needed to get back to the office. She figured she would drop by a local deli for a sandwich and take it back to the office while she finished some paperwork there.

James Simpson

Laura was so hungry by the time she got back to her office at 3 PM that she finished her sandwich before realizing she had started it. Just as she was about to begin some paperwork, her phone rang.

"This is Laura," she answered.

"Hi, we have not met, my name is James Simpson, I live across the breezeway from Brenda."

Sitting back in her chair, Laura took a deep breath, wondering just why James would suddenly be calling.

"I can't tell you if the person you are calling about is my client or not. But please tell me Brenda's last name and then tell me why you're calling."

"Well, I am calling to express some concern about Brenda Schneider, being that she has all her kids back and all. I get the feeling that she is overwhelmed. Honestly, I'm concerned about the kids."

"Why is that?", Laura asked.

"It's just that Brenda is so busy all the time trying to manage her kids and work, I'm afraid that they are not getting outside enough, being able to just be kids. I have a couple of kids of my own, so I know what it's like. After my wife died, I really had to make sure that I made time for them. My concern is that she just isn't quite able to do that right now."

Acting on intuition, Laura asked for some of James's identifying information. James was happy to provide his information, including his date of birth and social security number.

"Providing a good environment for children is extremely important. After my wife passed away, I had to move in with a friend of mine, and while it was certainly nice of him to let me and my kids live with him, he had his own kids he was taking care of, and things could get pretty chaotic. Anyways, I was just calling to express some concerns."

"Thanks for calling," Laura said and hung up.

Something about the conversation bothered Laura, although she couldn't identify what. But she couldn't sit here all day thinking about it, she needed to get to court for another case. She would have to check out his information when she got back.

Steven Holst

As Laura opened the door to the courthouse, a wind caught it and ripped it from her hands. She stepped inside and headed for courtroom. She kept reminding herself of all the little things she needed to do before the day was over. It seemed the day would never end.

As she entered the courtroom, she was going over the current case. This complicated case, which Laura inherited from a colleague, involved a man named Steven Holst who was accused of molesting his two daughters, Jane and Molly, now 14 and 16 years old. He was being arraigned in court and the two girls would also be there. They had been staying in a foster care home. Although Laura didn't know how comfortable they were at the courthouse, there wasn't much she could do about it. Plus, Laura had been in contact with Steven and the daughters since it all happened and felt she knew the girls well. Laura saw her supervisor sitting in the front row, right behind where the defendant, Steven, sat. Mary knew a little about the case, and was joining her there to provide any help she could.

"Been here long?" Laura asked as she sat down.

"No. Just got here actually. Do you know about Uncle Jimmy?", Mary asked.

"No, who's that?"

"Apparently he's not really their uncle, but that's how Steven's girls refer to him. He's been trying to get foster placement of the girls. With their dad going to jail and mom's rights having been terminated, I guess he plans to adopt them. He was living with them up until recently."

"Really. What do you think about it?" Laura asked.

"I don't like it. Steven claims that this 'Uncle Jimmy' also molested the girls, and while no evidence is there because the girls don't admit it, it's always a possibility. Of course, Steven could also be trying to point the finger somewhere else."

At this point, the judge entered. He saw Laura and Mary and acknowledged them with a nod.

"How does the defendant plea?" the judge asked.

"Guilty, your Honor," Steven's public defendant answered.

Back to the Office

Laura was drained. This whole day was a roller coaster. She had only a few things to do before she left for the day, one of which was check James's information. She logged into her computer and entered his social security number. As she began reading, her mouth involuntarily opened and her eyes widened.

"It can't be," she said out loud to herself.

James was Uncle Jimmy, there was no mistaking it. He was the one trying to get custody of Steven's girls. Of course it made sense. Earlier James had told her that he was living with a friend until recently. That friend was Steven. And now James was trying to get close to Brenda and Meredith, and both had young children. Laura stood up and started pacing her office, still in disbelief at the day's events. She must have paced for five minutes before she walked out of her office to go speak with Mary.

9   A Caring Heart

Charlotte Duron looked at her ringing phone. *Lynette?* She thought. *She must be wanting to give me an update after her respite shift at the Madison's home.*

"Hey, Lynette," she answered the phone. "How did it go at the Madison house?"

"Charlotte, Mr. Madison isn't home yet," Lynette stated, with anxiety in her voice. "He was supposed to be here like hours ago and he's still not home. I'm still here with Ms. Madison and Ryan, waiting. They are fine, but I don't know what's going on."

"Not home?" Charlotte repeated, puzzled. "And he didn't contact you or anything?" Mr. Madison had left for a doctor's appointment at 9:30 AM, leaving his wife with dementia and his son with Down syndrome in the care of the respite worker.

"No. I'm worried," Lynette answered. "What do you want me to do?"

"Well, if you can, stay a little longer and let me figure something out," Charlotte answered. "I'll call you back. I'm worried, too."

Tulsa, Oklahoma

As the second largest city in Oklahoma, Tulsa attracted a wide variety of residents. Tulsa's history included a history as a hub of the oil industry, a devastating race riot in 1921, and an iconic place on Route 66. Nestled on the Arkansas River in Northeastern Oklahoma, Tulsa enjoyed the region's lush greenery, state parks, and lakes. With a population of more than 600,000 people, almost 7% were Native American, 11% African American, and almost 12% Latino. Although on average, residents of Tulsa were slightly younger than other Oklahomans, the population of older adults was growing, approaching 13% of the city's population.

Northeastern Oklahoma Aging Alliance

The Northeastern Oklahoma Aging Alliance focused on caregiver support for several areas both in and outside of the Tulsa metro area, including Owasso, Sperry, and Catoosa. Funded by the Administration on Aging (AoA) within the US Department of Health and Human Services, the Alliance worked to carry out the spirit of the Older Americans Act of 1965 which promoted well-being of older adults through providing the services and programs to keep them independent in their homes and communities.

To fulfill this mission of working in the community to keep older adults out of nursing homes as long as possible, the Alliance focused on both client and caregiver support including providing housekeeping resources which helped with light housework, laundry, shopping, personal care, and meal preparation. Eligible clients could also receive in-home respite, case coordination, and transportation assistance. The Alliance offered nutritional assistance including delivered meals, health promotion educational programs, help with diabetes management, and assistance in creating greater accessibility and fall prevention in homes. As a designated Elder Abuse Provider Agency, the Alliance also investigated reports of elder abuse, including confinement, passive neglect, willful deprivation, and financial exploitation. Full assessments for the Medicaid waiver program were also provided, allowing eligible adults to receive nursing home level care within their own homes, covered by Medicaid.

The staff of approximately 15 included case managers with varying degrees, and three master's level social workers. Additionally, the Alliance contracted with many private companies or individuals for services in housekeeping or respite. In-home housekeepers or respite care workers all underwent extensive background checks, and the respite workers were all certified nursing assistants who were prepared to deal with emergencies if needed.

Charlotte Duron, MSW

Charlotte Duron was 24 when she graduated with her MSW from the University of Oklahoma in 2006. She had completed her foundation field placement at the Alliance the previous year as she had always loved working with older adults, so she was thrilled when they offered her a job as a caregiver specialist upon graduation. Inspired by her own experiences of watching her mother care for her grandfather who suffered from Alzheimer's disease, Charlotte was very patient and empathic to both the clients and caregivers coping with this devastating illness. Charlotte was a Caucasian woman with long, curly brown hair, a thin build, and an excellent work ethic. She was a diligent student and eager to accept responsibility. She and her husband, newly married, had recently bought a home in Tulsa, and were excited to start the new chapters of their adult lives.

As a caregiver specialist, Charlotte was charged with coordination of housekeeping services, respite, and caregiver support for the families served by the Alliance. Her direct supervisor, Ellen Potter, was a licensed social worker with more than 30 years of experience. Charlotte felt lucky because she was comfortable with Ellen and knew she could count on her for good advice. But she also felt a bit like a "lone wolf" as most of the other staff had positions that focused more on providing services to the client and Charlotte's position was purely supportive of the caregivers. Obviously, these roles overlapped, but

Charlotte was charged with seeing the task of supporting the caregiver as her priority.

Silas Madison

"Charlotte," called Melissa, one of the case managers. Melissa had a BSW and had been with the agency for several years. "Can I talk to you?"

"Sure," Charlotte answered, "come have a seat." She gestured towards the chair by her desk for Melissa to sit.

"I want to talk about the Madison family," Melissa began. "As you know, I've been doing the follow up case management visits out there for several months since Mr. Madison requested some help just with the upkeep. But I think they need some help from a caregiver specialist. He is no stranger to caregiving you know as he has been caring for his wife, Alma, ever since she was diagnosed with Alzheimer's disease almost six years ago. And their son, Ryan, has Down syndrome so he cares for them all. Ryan's in his 40s and works down at the Goodwill, but you know, he still needs lots of help."

"Right," Charlotte affirmed. "I know of this family. Silas Madison requested help with the housekeeping, but when we asked about respite care or any other type of service, he was kind of reticent to accept help right away. We have kept following up, but he says he just wants the housekeeping and he really appreciates it. The initial assessment with him though was done before I was here, so I haven't actually met him or the family yet. But I know his wife's dementia is pretty severe."

"Yes," Melissa continued. "Well, I'm worried about him. He doesn't look good. I'm worried that his own health is suffering, maybe because of the stress of taking care of both of them. He's had health problems in the past, but I'm really not getting much action from him on seeing a doctor himself. He always has a reason why he can't go. I wonder if you should go check it out. Maybe a caregiver specialist saying it would help convince him?"

"Sure," Charlotte agreed. "I'd love to meet him and see if a new start with me might encourage him to take advantage of more that we can offer."

Visiting the Madison Family

"We don't need anything," was the response when Charlotte contacted Mr. Madison on the phone, but he agreed to let Charlotte come visit. She drove through the South Tulsa neighborhood among a number of large, sprawling, newly constructed homes. *You can always spot the Alliance house from a mile away*, she thought to herself. *It's never the McMansion, but the overgrown ranch surrounded by these track houses in these new subdivisions and owned by the folks who stood their ground and refused to sell to the developers.* Sure enough, she found the address and the small, two-bedroom ranch home on a big lot, nestled between homes so big they almost overflowed their yard space. She walked to the front door.

Mr. Madison opened the door and smiled cautiously as Charlotte introduced herself. Charlotte immediately realized what Melissa was talking about. Mr. Madison's face was ashy, his clothes were too large and slightly stained, and he looked fatigued and worn, a little hunched over, and he seemed winded. His hand was cold when she shook it and she noticed his nails were slightly bluish in the nail beds. He was not a healthy man. He opened the door to allow her in.

"Thanks for letting me visit, Mr. Madison," Charlotte began. "You have a lovely home." The home was small, with wood paneling and shag carpet, but it was immaculately clean. Mr. Madison led her to the living room where his wife was sitting on the couch, which was covered with a plastic protector. *He seems to be doing a really good job keeping this place up, despite the fact that there are two people in this house that really require a lot of care*, thought Charlotte.

"Good morning, Mrs. Madison," Charlotte greeted her. The woman stared at her blankly. Charlotte noticed the small, slight woman in her 80s was clean, wearing a fresh nightgown, and her long white hair looked clean and brushed. She covered her lap with a pink crocheted blanket. "I'm here to see if there are things we can help your family with," Charlotte began.

"The nice boy brings me tea," she stated. Then she looked away and adjusted her blanket. She appeared to be referring to her husband as the "nice boy." Charlotte knew it was typical to forget names and relationships, but still have warm feelings towards loved ones.

"A cup of tea makes every day better," Charlotte responded, smiling kindly at the woman. She had read in the file that Mrs. Madison was not oriented to time or place, and that she no longer recognized her husband or son.

"We don't need help, we are doing fine." Mr. Madison stated flatly. He steered Charlotte towards the kitchen table and turned on the television for his wife to watch. Charlotte sat at the kitchen table and spoke gently with Mr. Madison.

"You are doing a wonderful job taking care of your wife, Mr. Madison," Charlotte stated. *This is a delicate conversation to have*, she thought to herself. *He seems like he feels kind of threatened, probably knowing he is barely holding this together and afraid I'll take his wife out of the house. But I want to help him see that his own health matters too if he is going to care for his family.*

"I'd like to hear more about your family," Charlotte began her assessment. "Since I am just meeting you all, I'm interested in hearing about what a typical day is for you." *I need to gather information about the wife's functioning and needs for care*, Charlotte thought. *But I also want information about Mr. Madison's health and the extent of his caregiving burden for both his wife and son.*

"Well," Mr. Madison began, "Alma watches her shows after I get her bathed and ready for the day. She needs the walker to get around the house, but she'll still fall if no one is helping her or try to sit and just fall on the ground. I walk along with her and kind of keep her going. She calls me 'the nice boy', you heard that. Kind of funny for an 86-year-old man to be called a nice boy," he chuckles a little but looks down at the table sadly. "But she knows she is home, and she knows her family loves her."

"She seems to trust you," Charlotte replied. "I know it is so difficult when someone you love is not well."

"She doesn't recognize our boy either, after spending her whole life caring for him. She was a teacher, but once Ryan was born and we knew he had Downs, she stayed home with him. He's a good boy, a sweet boy, just you know, couldn't pay a bill or fix a meal or do any of the stuff he needs to take care of himself. He stays here, and he loves her. He sits on the couch and watches TV with her, and she notices him, but I don't think she really knows who he is."

"Mr. Madison, your wife and your son are so lucky to have you to care for them," Charlotte stated after speaking with him for about an hour. "It is clear that you are taking such good care of your wife. Look at how well she is dressed and how clean your home is. You are really providing well for them." *Lots of complimenting might help build rapport with him*, Charlotte thought. *But I really mean it. He is taking good care of her, but at what cost to himself?* As the conversation continued, he warmed up and she learned about his history as a machinist, his service in World War II, and his wife's commitment to caring for their son. He seemed more comfortable with her, but she still had not been able to convince him further services may be worth considering.

"I know these conversations are really difficult, but they are crucial," Charlotte began as she sensed rapport building. "But I'm wondering what arrangements you have made for your son or your wife if something happened to you."

"Oh," he began, "I have a niece in Kansas. She'll step in if she needs to, and she'll make sure the family isn't split apart. I'm leaving everything to her anyway and she'll take care of Ryan too. That's my biggest fear is that someone will come in here and send Alma off to some godawful nursing home and put Ryan in some group home to rot."

"I'm glad your niece is there, and I can assure you that I don't want those things either," Charlotte responded. She glanced at the emergency contact in the file and confirmed the niece's name.

"But I guess what I'm worried about though is you," she continued. "If you aren't healthy and seeing your doctor, you won't be able to keep the pace of taking care of them. I'd really love to find someone to come stay with your wife just for a couple hours so you can see your doctor. You mentioned that you aren't feeling well yourself and have a history of trouble with congestive heart failure and high blood pressure. And that you've missed a few doctor's appointments since you didn't have anyone to help with Alma and Ryan," Charlotte stated gently. "I know it is hard to trust someone else to take care of her, even just for a little bit, but I really want to help. You can trust me to find someone to take good care of them so you can see your doctor and get a checkup."

"I do trust you," Mr. Madison stated, looking up at her. "I'll try it, just a couple hours couldn't hurt right?"

"Good," Charlotte said, smiling. "Let's make an appointment with your doctor and get something set up."

"Well, I can't do it this week because I have to pick up my son at his job tomorrow. And next week my wife has an appointment," he countered.

"We need to find a time that works, Mr. Madison," Charlotte said, making eye contact with him to try to express her seriousness. Charlotte waited with him while he called his doctor and set an appointment for the next Thursday, at 10:00 AM. Charlotte returned to the office to brief her supervisor.

Respite Begins

Charlotte contacted Lynette Hart, CNA, to provide respite for Mr. Madison. Lynette had experience working with folks with developmental disabilities, so she seemed like a good choice to help this family. Lynette was an African American woman in her late 40s, whom Charlotte found to be a person with solid judgment, compassionate, even keeled, and took things in her stride. She was one of the more seasoned respite workers, and Charlotte and Ellen both had lots of confidence in her.

"Huh, how weird!" Lynette had exclaimed when Charlotte called her to set up the respite visit. "I actually know their son, Ryan! He probably won't remember me, but I met him at the Goodwill when I was a caregiver for this other boy who worked there. My client and Ryan were kind of friends. I remember him, he was a sweet kid."

"That's great, Lynette, it seems serendipitous!" Charlotte exclaimed. "I think this will work out fine. Just be there at 9:30 AM tomorrow, so Mr. Madison can make it to his appointment at 10."

The Next Afternoon, 2 PM

Charlotte Duron looked at her ringing phone. *Lynette?* She thought. *She must be wanting to give me an update after her respite shift at the Madison's home.*

"Hey, Lynette," she answered the phone. "How did it go at the Madison house?"

"Charlotte, Mr. Madison isn't home yet," Lynette stated, anxiety in her voice. "He was supposed to be here like hours ago and he's still not home. I'm still here with Ms. Madison and Ryan, waiting. They are fine, but I don't know what's going on."

"Not home?" Charlotte repeated, puzzled and surprised. "And he didn't contact you or anything?" Mr. Madison had left for his doctor's appointment at 9:30 AM.

"No. I'm worried," Lynette answered. "What do you want me to do?"

"Well, if you can, stay a little longer and let me figure something out. I can authorize you to stay a couple more hours," Charlotte answered. "I'll call you back. I'm worried, too."

Charlotte remembered the name of the doctor Mr. Madison mentioned, Dr. Whelan. She looked up his number, dialed, and asked for Dr. Whelan's nurse.

"I know you can't tell me much because of HIPAA," Charlotte began when the phone was answered, "but a client of mine, Silas Madison, was seen there this morning." Charlotte explained her role as a social worker for the family. "We have a respite worker out there staying with his wife and son saying he hasn't returned, and well, we are really worried."

"Uh, well," the nurse answered uncomfortably, "you are right I can't say much I guess. But sometimes when calls like this happen I tell people they should call the hospitals, you know, like maybe St. John's hospital."

"OK, um, thanks." Charlotte responded slowly, puzzled. She called the hospital, and repeated the story to the operator, who transferred her to another extension.

"Cardiac nursing, this is Betsy," stated the woman who answered the phone. Charlotte repeated the story.

"Let me put you on hold a minute," Betsy stated. Charlotte waited, anxiously, almost 20 minutes.

"OK, I'm back," Betsy finally returned, slightly out of breath. "I went and talked to him and got consent to talk to you. He can't talk himself, he's on oxygen."

"What happened?" Charlotte asked, nervously.

"I guess he went to see his doctor and the doctor realized right away that he was having severe heart problems. He had congestive heart failure and there was lots of fluid around his heart. They called an ambulance and by the time he got here it was in the midst of a heart attack. He's stabilized now, but not breathing well, and still has lots of fluid. He's resting, but he's in critical condition."

Charlotte thanked the nurse for the information and hung up. *I guess I need to make arrangements for the night, and then I'll go out there first thing in the morning and visit him. Maybe he will feel better and we can call his niece to come help us.* Charlotte called her supervisor, Ellen, and brought her up to date on the story and received authorization to pay Lynette for an overnight shift. *I just hope she can do it*, Charlotte thought as she called Lynette.

"Lynette, can you stay for the night? We don't have the biggest respite budget, but this is an emergency so we can figure out how to pay you for the hours," she asked after bringing Lynette up to date.

"Sure," Lynette agreed. "I'm able to stay a while."

Charlotte looked up the niece's phone number in the Madison file and dialed. The phone rang and rang, and finally went to voice mail. Charlotte left an urgent message for the niece to call her immediately.

The Next Morning, 8 AM

Charlotte stopped at the office briefly the next morning, hoping to check her email before she headed to the hospital. As she sat down at her desk and turned on her computer, her phone rang. She recognized the number as St. John's hospital.

"Charlotte? It's Betsy from St. John's cardiac," Betsy said. "I'm so sorry, but Mr. Madison passed during the night. After we spoke on the phone, he slipped into a coma and he expired about 3:30 AM."

"Oh no," Charlotte said sadly. She closed her eyes a moment to try to stop her tears. *That poor family*, she thought.

"Charlotte, do you have an emergency contact for him though?" Betsy continued. "I tried to call this niece that is in the file when he first got here, but there is no answer. I can't find any other contact and I haven't been able to reach her."

"Yes," Charlotte responded, "I have left a message too, but maybe there is a different number." She read off the phone number from the Madison file.

"That's what I have," stated Betsy. "No answer."

Charlotte ended the call and sat quietly at her desk. Her thoughts were circling wildly and she was starting to feel sick to her stomach. *If we can't get hold of a family member right away, what is going to happen to Mrs. Madison and Ryan? I don't have the budget to keep a respite worker there much longer. Am I going to have to make arrangements for them? And he trusted me to keep his family together! Do I need to make arrangements for his body? And … am I going to have to explain this to them? What will I say?*

10 Judge Not

"It's contrary for that child to be in his home," Judge Michael Pond exclaimed. "The child is to be placed back with her maternal grandmother. And it's my responsibility to report the father to immigration." It was March 2008, with Judge Pond presiding over a Commerce, Oklahoma deprivation case.

Foster care worker Goldie Long was stunned. She sometimes thought Judge Pond was erratic, but this was outrageous. She turned to her colleague, Susan Youngburn, who appeared equally shocked, and mouthed the words, "Can he do that?!"

Commerce, Oklahoma and House Bill 1804

Located in rural Ottawa County, off historic U.S. Highway 66, Commerce was the childhood home of Mickey Mantle. Named after the Commerce Mining and Royalty Company, it was a mining town until most mines closed by 1960, and residents turned to farming and ranching. In 1983 it was designated a U.S. Environmental Protection Agency Superfund Site due to the pollution caused by mining (Oklahoma Historical Society, 2007). By 2008, 5% of employment was in agriculture, 20% in manufacturing, and 25% in educational, health, and social services. According to the U.S. Census, the total population of Commerce was less than 3000, with 68% white, 19% Hispanic, and <1% black. Fifteen percent of families had income below the poverty level. While the percentage of children in poverty dropped from 28 to 24 in Ottawa County between 1990 and 2000, it remained higher than the state percentage of 20.

In 2007, both state legislators who represented Commerce were Democrats, and both voted for House Bill 1804 which created the Oklahoma Taxpayer and Citizen Protection Act of 2007. The Act went into law in November 2007 and was meant to combat illegal immigration. It had been characterized as the toughest law on immigration in the U.S.

Oklahoma Department of Human Services—Child Protective Services

Child Protective Services (CPS) were provided by the Children and Family Service Division (CFSD) of the Oklahoma Department of Human Services.

There were six units within CFSD: Administrative Services; Permanency, Adoptions, and Independent Living; Continuous Quality Improvement; Protection, Services and Training; Resources; and Technology and Governance. CPS was under the Protection, Services and Training unit. CPS policy mandated that all child protection workers—including investigation, foster care, and adoption—work closely as a team.

In September, 2008, CPS accepted 2116 abuse and/or neglect referrals for investigation from across the state. Sixteen of these were in Ottawa County, where Commerce was located.

Statewide, many children removed from their parents were placed in kinship care, i.e., out-of-home placements with their relatives. Sometimes children went to kinship care immediately and then moved to other foster care arrangements and sometimes they first went to non-kin foster care and then moved to kinship.

Goldie Long

Goldie Long began working for the Oklahoma Department of Protective and Family Services in 2000 as a protective services investigator and then, in 2003, as a foster care worker. Because the agency would pay for her education, she decided to seek further education. While continuing to work, Goldie entered the MSW program at the University of Oklahoma-Tulsa and committed to remain at the agency at least two more years following graduation. She graduated with the MSW in December of 2007. Goldie was young, petite, white, and unintimidating, but could also convey a "no-nonsense" attitude. Colleagues described her as unflappable. Covering two rural counties could be exhausting work, especially because Goldie was so thorough.

Judge Pond

Judge Pond was the only county judge in Ottawa County. He presided over many types of cases, including deprived children, criminal, juvenile, and civil. His knowledge of the law was broad and deep, he was diligent in trying to follow the law, and he was proud of his work. In his late 50s, Judge Pond was a short, balding, slightly overweight white man. Goldie came to know him as an unusual personality. Court was supposed to start at 9:30 AM, but it never started before 10:15. He often sat in his office area, telling random stories about his childhood fishing, or his son's activities, or his weekend with his grandkids, all while the parents were sitting out in the lobby area waiting for court to start. Sometimes he wouldn't even go into the courtroom; if it was a review with no changes and everyone was in consensus, he announced in his office instead of chambers, "Well, good, everyone is in agreement. The kid will stay where she is. The parents are kind of moving along, not doing much, but just enough to keep them going. Set the next date for three months." Recently, some attorneys had started requesting formal proceedings in chambers, and the judge complied with no complaint.

Goldie felt like she had a good relationship with Judge Pond. She first worked with him as an investigation worker. She didn't usually testify or actually interact in many court hearings now that she worked in foster care, but if there was something related to a child placement she would testify. Judge Pond often asked her, "Why don't you come back? Why don't you want to do investigations anymore?" Goldie always thought to herself, *Because I don't want to visit your courtroom*, but said aloud, "Foster care is better hours." Judge Pond relied on Goldie for advice about a number of non-CPS topics. For example, he called her to ask questions related to guardianship or custody in civil cases. On a few occasions, he called Goldie to ask if she could help get a private home study done for his acquaintances, or asked her to come to court to speak with families about available social services. She always told him it wasn't her job, but she did it anyway, for the sake of good relations.

Judge Pond was infamous for disregarding CPS policy. Goldie remembered hearing a story of the CPS County Director trying to give the judge a copy of a new policy that CPS was implementing, to which Judge Pond responded, "Oh, thanks. You can hang on to that for me."

Additionally, Judge Pond was unpredictable. Sometimes he would threaten parents with termination even though the children weren't in CPS custody. Other children could be in custody for years with no parental contact, and he would avoid termination, saying, "Well, you know they seem like they might be motivated to do something." Sometimes he seemed more sympathetic towards grandparents than parents. Occasionally, Goldie was pleasantly surprised when the judge accepted her recommendations without a fuss. Goldie never quite knew how he would rule.

Baby Olivia's Story and the Home Visits

Cindy Reyes was 29 years old when she gave birth to Olivia in September, 2008; both tested positive for cocaine. The hospital staff told Cindy not to breastfeed, but observed her breastfeeding several times. The staff also twice found Olivia lying face-down on a pillow, at risk for suffocation. Each time, Cindy explained, "She just rolled over." The hospital made a referral to CPS, and the investigation worker got a court order taking Olivia into CPS custody, and giving physical custody to Cindy's mother, Paulla Reyes. Goldie was then assigned as the foster worker, and made an appointment to assess the family in the Reyes' home the next week.

Goldie reviewed Cindy's records before her first visit with Paulla to start the foster care certification process. It was a file thick with information on Cindy's problems and her other three children. Cindy had been in and out of jail on drug and drug-related charges such as theft and larceny. She had no source of income. Her other three children (fathered by three men who had no contact or involvement with the children) stayed with Paulla. The three children were never in CPS custody because Cindy signed over guardianship to Paulla.

At the home visit, Paulla opened the door. She was a short, dark-haired and dark-complected Mexican-American and 56 years old. Although English was not her first language, she spoke it fluently, but had trouble reading it. Her parents, now deceased, were Mexican immigrants and farm laborers. Paulla had picked cotton as a child, and now worked on a factory assembly line. Paulla showed Goldie around the small, tidy house. Olivia was asleep in her crib and the other three children were clean and playing outside in the pleasant weather.

Just as they were sitting down to do the extensive paperwork required for foster care certification, a woman unexpectedly walked into the house, wearing a sheer blouse. Paulla yelled at her, "Why are you wearing that?! I can't believe you are wearing that in my house!"

"I'm grown," the woman hissed, "and I can wear whatever I want!"

While they argued, Goldie wondered, *Is this Cindy? What's she doing here? She doesn't look at all like she's ever had kids, let alone just given birth.*

"I get that you are Paulla's daughter, but which daughter are you?" Goldie asked. "Are you the mother of Olivia or who exactly are you?"

"Yes," she huffed, "I'm Cindy, Olivia's mother."

"I'm Goldie Long, Olivia's foster care worker," Goldie responded. "I'm here to fill out papers to certify your mother as a foster care parent for Olivia. I wasn't expecting you, but it's no problem for you to be here while I explain the process and the paperwork to your mother."

As the three women sat down at the kitchen table to begin the paperwork, Goldie thought, *She's very attractive—looks like she's 19 years old—but you just know those years of drug use are creeping up on her and she's going to look bad in a few years. She's not really unkempt, but you can tell she doesn't take care of herself. You know she doesn't get much good sleep with all that police activity.*

Goldie began by going over the first form with Paulla. Twenty minutes later, the children came in from outside, each trying to crawl into Paulla's lap. Paulla gave them candy, saying, "Grandma can't play with you right now. Cindy, can't you watch them for a second while I'm doing this?"

Cindy half-tended to the girls while also asking questions, "Now what about this? It has a lot in there about 'can you protect the children from the parents.' What does that mean?"

"It's up to your worker," Goldie explained, "and it's going to depend on how you're progressing in your treatment plan. How much you see your kids is going to depend on if you do what's in your plan or if you go against what you've been told to do."

The visit turned into a very chaotic two hours. To Goldie, Paulla seemed a bit scatter-brained and flustered by all the child activity. Goldie had to explain most of the paperwork more than once so that she was sure Paulla understood because of the chaos and because many kinship/foster parents don't quite understand that their role is not as grandparent. Goldie covered all the "rules": Goldie and Olivia's worker, Susan Youngburn, a child welfare specialist, would be visiting at least once a month; Paulla would be required to take Olivia on weekly supervised visits with Cindy, eventually that could occur in Paulla's home; Paulla would have to report to Goldie how well the visits went, how well Cindy was bonding with Olivia; Paulla nor anyone else would be allowed to spank any of the children.

Towards the end of the two hours, Cindy picked up Paulla's cell phone, and Paulla said to her, "I wish you wouldn't use my cell phone all the time. You don't pay for it and you don't help pay for anything with the kids."

"Why would you say that in front of her?" Cindy asked, pointing towards Goldie, "saying I'm using your phone all time?! That's not how that is. Why are you telling them that I am over here all the time?"

"I'm not going to lie to them. You are here all the time." At that, Cindy stomped out of the house without another word.

"I thought she'd grow up some day," Paulla sighed. "She's 29 years old and has four kids and nothing's changed."

After the paperwork was finished, Olivia finally woke up. Paulla immediately picked her up and started heating a bottle. Goldie noted that their interactions were good, and Paulla said, "I want you to know that I take very good care of Olivia. She can stay here forever. If you need to look closer at anything in the house, you can. I'll do whatever you say. Anytime you want to come over you can."

Goldie explained that she would visit as much as Susan would, and sometimes they would come together. She added, "I'm a bit concerned about your ability to protect Olivia, Paulla, with Cindy coming in and out of the house like this."

"I never leave Olivia or any of the kids alone with Cindy. She's not allowed in the house if she's high or drunk. I can protect Olivia. I've been taking care of the other kids with no problems, so you know I can do it." Still, Goldie wasn't entirely convinced that Cindy couldn't manipulate Paulla.

Because Paulla was not yet an approved foster parent, Goldie and Susan made a joint home visit a week later. Again, Cindy showed up. While Susan questioned Cindy about how often she visited, Goldie thought, *It's weird to me that they didn't take the other kids into custody. It surprises me that Judge Pond wouldn't want them all taken into custody.*

Cindy had given Susan the name and contact information of Olivia's biological father just hours after Olivia's birth. Now Susan wanted to further explore how Cindy felt about him. "How would you feel about Rodolfo beginning visits next week?"

"He can visit Olivia, but I don't want him around my other girls. Those are not his children and I don't feel like any man should be alone with them unless it's their father."

Cindy soon exited the house, and her oldest daughter entered, home via bus from kindergarten. The girl immediately went to the refrigerator and pulled out a gallon of milk. While trying to lift it to her mouth, she dropped it on the floor, spilling a three-foot swath of milk. Paulla sighed and said, "I told you, you cannot do that. You cannot go into the refrigerator unless you ask me."

Paulla began cleaning up the spill and the girl began wailing. "I told you," Paulla repeated, "I told you not to get into the refrigerator unless I tell you. I'm gonna fix you a snack as soon as the ladies leave. You didn't listen to me, so you are going to have to sit here until we are done."

The wailing continued for another 40 minutes. Paulla just ignored it but it was difficult for Goldie to do so. *Paulla is already overwhelmed with three children, she thought. It might be good if Rodolfo turns out to be interested. She left that day thinking, This isn't a bad placement, but I wish things would improve.*

Olivia's Father, Rodolfo Madrigal

Susan met Olivia's biological father, Rodolfo Madrigal, the week after Olivia was born. When she returned to the office, Susan stopped to talk with Goldie:

"Rodolfo is 21 years old. Physically, he's a little guy and he's been working outdoors on a chicken farm for three years, so he's really dark-skinned. His English is okay, but sometimes I don't understand him and I'm not sure he always understands me. He was nervous at first about contact with me because he assumed we'd call immigration. I had to reassure him every way I could that I *don't care* about his legal status. I guess he finally believed me because he said he would like custody of Olivia. Olivia is his first kid. He lives with his aunt and has not seen Cindy since before Olivia was born. I'm feeling really optimistic about this placement, Goldie."

Susan devised a treatment plan for Rodolfo that included parenting classes. Rodolfo was extremely compliant. In December, a couple months later, Susan bounced into Goldie's office.

"This dad is great. He's done everything I said and you should see him with Olivia! He is so in love with her and I think he's going to make a great dad. I'm recommending that Olivia be placed with him." Goldie was pleased and relieved as well.

Cindy is Out of the Picture

Cindy had a reunification plan that required she attend parenting classes, get a substance abuse evaluation, obtain a stable income and home for at least six months, and participate in comprehensive in-home treatment. But Cindy never took the first step towards getting Olivia back. Over the next three months, Cindy got arrested three or four more times for drug-related charges. Goldie never understood how, but Cindy was always released after a week. Goldie remained a bit uneasy about Paulla's ability to protect Olivia, with Cindy's constant coming and going. Then one day Cindy stole Paulla's car and a large amount of money, at which point Paulla turned Cindy into the police. Cindy did not get out of jail that time, and Goldie felt a little more confidence in Paulla. However, she felt the best placement was with Rodolfo.

The Judge's Decisions

In January 2008, much to Paulla's dismay, Judge Pond placed Olivia in a trial reunification with Rodolfo based on Susan's recommendation. Paulla had cooperated with Rodolfo's visits, but she was adamantly against his taking custody. "She's my grandchild," she told Judge Pond, "and I want her with me and the other kids. Olivia should not be with him. I'm planning on quitting my job so I can get welfare and be home with Olivia."

Goldie, however, felt good about the decision. *Paulla's doing okay with the kids. They are safe. But I just don't understand why we would place an extra burden on this grandmother who has three kids when dad is perfectly fine.*

In March, the case came before Judge Pond again for review. Judge Pond started reading through Susan's report:

> Cindy is currently incarcerated pending criminal charges. Her attorney states that she may get up to eight years if convicted. She has completed absolutely none of her treatment plan. Rodolfo has proven to be a very good, nurturing father. His girlfriend and aunt have also bonded very well with Olivia. His employer is so impressed with his work that he is trying to get him a work visa, with the employer as Rodolfo's sponsor.

"Wait a minute. Wait a minute." Judge Pond looked startled. "This father is here illegally?! I didn't know that. It's contrary for that child to be in his home. The child is to be placed back with her maternal grandmother. And it's my responsibility to report the father to immigration."

Goldie was stunned. Her office had reunified children with noncustodial parents who lived in Mexico, and immigration status was never an issue. *Rodolfo is a great placement, a great parent. Placing Olivia with Paulla is a mistake! How can I fix this mess?*

Reference

Oklahoma Historical Society. (2007). Commerce. Retrieved January 2, 2010, from http://digital.library.okstate.edu/encyclopedia/entries/C/CO037.html

11 Disastrous

After the Houston city council meeting, at which The Metropolitan Organization (TMO) leaders "testified" about all the problems being experienced by TMO family, friends and neighbors, three TMO leaders and two organizers waited outside Mayor Turner's door.

"That city council meeting last week got kind of intense," said Sheyda. "Do you think we offended the mayor?"

"He seemed pretty upset," Paula, a leader from Fifth Ward Missionary Baptist, replied. "He kept saying he cares about the people—'I don't want anyone to be heartbroken!' Yet we're not seeing much action on his part. I think he needed to hear our stories to get a better picture of what people are dealing with. The story you shared with him about Lena was perfect; it's too bad she was too ill to tell it herself."

"I hope it got our point across, that people are confused and don't know what to do. The city really needs to be more involved in helping people," Ruby said. "I hope our meeting today can clear some things up with the mayor, and that our relationship hasn't been damaged too much."

Several minutes later Mayor Turner opened his office door.

"Hello, everyone. Come on in," he said.

The women walked into his office and saw there was another guest present.

"This is Tom, the Housing and Development Coordinator," Mayor Turner said. "I've asked him to join us today. I've got something I'd like to share with all of you about an encounter I had recently."

Sheyda, Paula, Ruby, and the others sat up straight, curious to hear what he had to say.

"So, last week I was on my lunch break and decided to go to Whataburger. While I was in the drive-through, the cashier recognized me as the mayor and told me about his mom, who had not yet received any help on her house. I told the man to write down her information and that I would pass it on to our Housing and Development Coordinator." He paused and looked at Tom. "So, Tom, here you go!" he said, handing him a piece of paper. "I'd like for you to contact this woman today and see what we can do to get some repairs going on her house."

Tom took the paper. "Yes sir! I will give her a call this afternoon."

"So," said Mayor Turner, looking at Sheyda and Paula, "I wanted to share this with you to let you know that I'm going to be doing more to get people the help they need."

Ruby and Sheyda gave each other a side glance. *So, is that what it takes for people to get help from the city?!* Sheyda thought. *They need to have a personal connection or encounter with the mayor himself?!*

Houston, Texas and Harvey

Just prior to Hurricane Harvey, almost 2.5 million people lived in Houston, a city where almost 21% of people fell below the poverty level. Over half of the residents were white (58%), almost a quarter were black (23%), and 44% of residents were Hispanic or Latino (U.S. Census Bureau, 2016).

The Greater Third Ward area in Houston was hit hard by Harvey. It was home to over 14000 people and was a predominantly black neighborhood where just over half of the residents made less than $25,000 per year (City of Houston Planning and Development Department, 2017a).

Also traumatized by Harvey was the Greater Fifth Ward in Houston. Nearly half of the residents were Hispanic and the other half black, and 56% of residents earned less than $25000 per year (City of Houston Planning and Development Department, 2017b).

The Industrial Areas Foundation and The Metropolitan Organization

Founded in 1940, the Industrial Areas Foundation (IAF) remains the largest organizing institute in the U.S. The IAF works with thousands of religious congregations, nonprofits, civic organizations, and unions in over 65 cities across the country to promote broad-based organizing projects at the local level.

The Metropolitan Organization (TMO) in Houston is part of the West/Southwest IAF regional network and the IAF national network. Formed in 1980, TMO exists to give voice to people about major decisions affecting their lives. As of 2018, TMO consisted of 40 church congregations from Houston and surrounding areas and a few nonprofits, though in the past it also had unions and schools. The organization has historically focused on four main issues: immigration, work, health, and education. TMO employed three professional organizers whose primary responsibility was to develop and teach volunteers how to be effective, civic leaders so that they may take action for their communities.

Sheyda Zakerion Brown

Sheyda's parents emigrated to the U.S. from Iran before she was born and growing up she helped her parents at their family-owned restaurant. Upon graduating from the University of Oklahoma with a BSW at age 22, she immediately entered the MSW program, graduating in 2017. While in school, she was involved with the local IAF and enjoyed the advocacy work and community broad-based organizing. She applied for a job with IAF and was offered a position as a junior organizer with TMO in Houston, Texas. She was assigned to two zones in Houston: the Fifth Ward area and the Third Ward area where she worked with two lead organizers, Martin Davis and Ruby Diaz.

Sheyda had been working with TMO for about three months before Hurricane Harvey hit. During the hurricane, she had gone to stay with a friend approximately 30 minutes north of Houston in a fourth-floor apartment that narrowly missed being damaged by the storm; however, the torrential rains flooded the surrounding area and she could not travel more than two miles from that apartment for a week. Her personal encounter with the storm and the stories she heard from co-workers and friends increased her awareness of the challenges Houston residents faced in their recovery.

The Impacts of Hurricane Harvey

Sheyda kept in touch with her MSW cohort and often spoke or texted with some of them. She was heading out the door, when one called. "Hey, what's up?" Holly asked.

"Oh, I'm on my way to speak with a congregant in one of our parishes. I'm really frustrated. But I keep forgetting to ask you, have you read that article in the January 2018, issue of *The New Yorker*, by Lawrence Wright? I think it's called 'The Glut Economy'?" (Wright, 2018).

"I haven't."

Sheyda promised to send it to her. "It just makes me so angry. Like that article in *Texas Tribune* from August 31, 2017 I sent you, and all the stories we are hearing from our leaders. All the red tape, the right hand doesn't know what the left hand is doing, and none of our people are getting help. I gotta go or I'll be late to this woman's house."

"Hang in there! At least you're doing something!"

"This is Worse Than the Cancer"

Sheyda walked up to one of the houses in her ward. She had recently met someone who was related to the woman living in this house, Lena Tindall, and learned Lena was one of the 200 cases TMO helped shepherd to Catholic Charities in September. The relative mentioned Lena had not received a single call from a caseworker and that her home was in desperate need of repair. Sheyda knocked on the door and a small woman with spiked hair, who looked to be in her 70s or 80s, opened the door.

"Hi, my name is Sheyda. I work with The Metropolitan Organization and I've come to speak with you about your house. May I come in?"

"Oh, yes, thank you for coming" Lena said. "Come on in."

Sheyda followed Lena through stacks of boxes into the living room, which was crowded with more boxes. Sheyda surveyed the empty spaces where walls used to be and the exposed insulation where sheetrock had been removed. Mold covered portions of the walls and ceiling, and the stench was almost overwhelming.

"How are you doing?" Sheyda asked.

"Oh, ok," Lena replied. "I'm glad to be back in my house. I've stayed with friends and relatives for the past few months, and I appreciate their hospitality, I really do, but staying with them just doesn't feel the same as being in my own home." Her eyes filled with tears. "I've lived in this house over 40 years. It's all I've got. I can't bear the thought of leaving."

Sheyda looked at the frail, elderly woman across from her, wondering at the pain she must feel. "I know it must be hard," she said, "trying to pick up the pieces and move forward after the hurricane. I understand your home needs repairs and that you haven't heard from anybody about getting them taken care of. I'd like to know what aid you've applied for and if you've received anything."

Lena turned towards Sheyda, her brow furrowed. "I don't know, I think I got maybe $1500 from FEMA. But I don't know, I don't know what I'm doing..." She turned and gazed wistfully out the window. "All I know is that I'm not going to live to see my home fixed, and this is worse than the stage four cancer."

Sheyda's stomach sunk. *This is no condition for an elderly woman to live in, let alone someone with cancer. I know funerals are way up in the senior community in this neighborhood due to stress and health concerns. What can TMO do to make sure this woman, and others like her, get the help they need?* "I'll see what I can do, Lena, and get back with you."

Still Waiting...

Later that day, Sheyda and her supervisor, Ruby, were sorting through their files and notes about TMO's hurricane relief efforts since Harvey hit.

"According to our records," Ruby said, "TMO trained about 30 leaders with Catholic Charities to conduct intakes with hurricane survivors at their parishes. Altogether, the leaders submitted 200 intakes to Catholic Charities. It's been seven months, and most of those clients haven't heard from a case manager!"

"That's a long time to wait," Sheyda said. "I heard Catholic Charities had received over 5000 intakes in total and only had ten case managers hired. No wonder it's taking so long!"

Ruby had an idea. "Why don't you call Billy Hutton to get some insight from him? He was a TMO organizer during Hurricane Katrina before we were all at TMO and he's now in Baton Rouge. I know the circumstances were very different, but I'm curious to know more about TMO's recovery work after that storm."

Sheyda returned to her cubicle, dialed the number and waited.

"Hello, this is Billy."

"Hi Billy, it's Sheyda Brown from TMO." Sheyda explained the reasons for her call and the situation with Catholic Charities. "I'm feeling a bit overwhelmed by TMO's work with Harvey and I'm curious to know what you did after Katrina. Do you have some time to talk?"

"Sure, I've got a few minutes. What would you like to know?"

"I know TMO was pretty involved in helping survivors of Hurricane Katrina, even though almost none of them were from Houston. Could you tell me what some of the things were you all did to help?"

"Well, we did a lot. You might know this, but nearly a quarter-million people came from Louisiana seeking refuge in Houston after Katrina. Just three weeks later, though, Hurricane Rita hit the Gulf area, so even more came. With so many people seeking shelter here, we helped organize evacuees in the Astrodome by designating a playground for children and secure areas for the elderly. Also, you can imagine how desperate people were to use their phones during this time, so we persuaded the Federal Communications Commission to maintain evacuees' cell phone service even if they fell behind in their bills."

"That's really incredible!" Sheyda exclaimed.

"It really was. It definitely helped that we had so much support from Mayor Bill White, who invited me to attend their daily strategy sessions on disaster planning," said Billy.

"It's great that TMO was able to do all of that right after the hurricane," said Sheyda. "Our problem with Harvey is that, seven months later, we've got all these people who are still waiting to receive help. There seems to be a lot of money floating around, but it's not getting to the people who need it, at least not very quickly."

"Give Steve Snider a call," advised Billy. "He was a leader from Resurrection who was heavily involved. He may have more insight."

"What's Going to Make TMO Stronger for the Future?"

The next Monday, Sheyda sat at her desk and stared at her inbox filled with unopened messages. Her mind was turning over the conversations she'd had over the past week including Lena and the many other senior citizens in the community who had to live in moldy homes, many of them with pre-existing health conditions. She couldn't bear the thought of these people having to suffer terrible conditions when their health was already vulnerable.

Her thoughts were interrupted when Martin, Sheyda's other supervisor, and Ruby entered her cubicle.

"Hi, Sheyda. How's it going? We brought you some lunch from Taquito's." Martin handed her some vegetarian tacos.

"Oh, I was just thinking about the challenges people are facing in getting the home repairs they need and wondering what our role should be in all of this. You know, before the hurricane, we were just starting to brainstorm strategies to get people to the polls for the upcoming election. With the hurricane we've had to channel all our energy into helping victims recover, but our capacity is limited and I'm wondering what's the best thing for us to focus on."

"I'm really frustrated with the logjam that Greater Houston Community Foundation is overseeing." Ruby drummed her fingers on the table. "The mayor and county judge raised funds and turned them over to GHCF to be distributed. GHCF also raised funds. Their responsibility is to coordinate how the money will be used for relief work. The agencies created the Coordinated Access Network as a way for case managers to hold information on persons needing recovery help in one place. They formed an online intake process to gather information so services would not be duplicated. Additionally, the organizations trained case managers from hundreds of nonprofits to go out and conduct case management for those affected by the storm. The Red Cross, United Way, and BakerRipley are all involved, but I'm not sure how. They all sound like good ideas, but where's the oversight?! And with so much money and resources, why aren't our folks getting help?!"

"You raise some good points," Martin said. "I've been wondering what more we can do to help get money to the people who need it, especially our people—those who are low-income, seniors, or without documents. There is money here already, but there is also a lot of money tied up at the federal level."

"Right," said Ruby. "I was thinking about whether we should take our leaders to the federal government and fight them for the money, since it's taking so long to get here."

"But is that worth our energy, and we have to ask ourselves whether we even have enough power to go after those folks," Martin mused.

"I've wondered some of those same things," said Sheyda, as she wiped some avocado off her fingers. "Ultimately, how long should we focus on this? Are we fighting a losing battle and just frustrating our leaders? What is going to make TMO stronger for the future?" She let out a long, exasperated sigh. "Unfortunately, I don't know the answer at this point."

"There Aren't Any Case Managers..."

Furthering her "research" and following Billy's advice, Sheyda sat with her cup of tea at a small, square table in the corner of the coffee shop across from Steve Snider.

"Thanks for meeting with me, Steve. It's really great to be able to get some perspective from you about what TMO should try to do after this awful storm."

"I'm happy to meet with you, Sheyda. Tell me what you've learned so far about the needs of people living in your community."

"Well, first off," Sheyda said, "the timing of the storm could not have been worse. Since it hit right near the start of a new month, many of the residents in my wards have had difficulty paying their rent due to wages lost from missed work."

"Yes, the financial impact on residents after something like this can be incredibly hard. What else have you learned?" Steve asked.

"So, this seems crazy to me, but apparently if you accept help for home repairs from one agency, it disqualifies you from receiving help from another agency. I don't quite understand this. Can you explain that?"

Steve nodded his head. "Yes, so as you've learned, people can receive services for home repairs from the city, nonprofits, or FEMA, but not all of them. The problem is, say somebody needs $40,000 in home repairs but they don't know that the city's program provides up to $60,000, so they accept FEMA's $20,000 because it's the first thing they heard about and they've been waiting a long time for help. Now they have $20,000 but they need to come up with on their own to pay for the remaining repairs because the city only helps those with no FEMA funds, when they might have been eligible to receive help from the city that would have covered all of the repairs."

"What's so terrible about that," Sheyda replied, "is many of the people we work with come from low-income homes, so they are already struggling financially. It seems like they're being further victimized by not having this knowledge available to them, which could prevent them from taking on debt to repair their homes."

"Right," said Steve. "The problem is there aren't any case managers available who can tell people which program will benefit them the most depending on what kind of repairs they need, so people are just accepting the first help they can find."

"Something else we're learning," Sheyda said, "is that some people are being denied help from FEMA for various reasons. Does that mean they're disqualified from receiving any help from FEMA?"

"Not exactly," said Steve. "What people see as a denial, FEMA sees as the beginning of a relationship. But people don't know this and don't know that they can—and should—appeal."

Sheyda's eyebrows raised. "You mean it's possible for people to still get help after being denied by FEMA, they just need to appeal?"

"Yep," said Steve. "From what I understand, individuals can advocate for themselves by calling or writing to FEMA and explaining which program they think they qualify for. It's not a great system, but that's the way it is."

"I had no idea," said Sheyda. "Thanks for explaining all of this, Steve!"

"No problem! I wish it wasn't such a messy process. People are already confused as it is and trying to figure out how to move forward after such a devastating disaster. That's where TMO comes in and gets to help make the process less confusing."

"You're right," said Sheyda. "That's why I'm trying to figure this all out for myself, so I know how to explain it to those who need the help!"

Later that week, Ruby and Martin met with Sheyda to start strategizing about their next steps. They decided to get on the agenda for the next city council meeting. "OK, so I'll get us on the agenda, and pull together some leaders to develop scripts and plan turnout," Sheyda said.

Meeting with the Mayor

After the Houston city council meeting, at which The Metropolitan Organization (TMO) leaders "testified" about all the problems being experienced by

TMO family, friends, and neighbors, three TMO leaders and two organizers waited outside Mayor Turner's door.

"That city council meeting last week got kind of intense," said Sheyda. "Do you think we offended the mayor?"

"He seemed pretty upset," Paula, a leader from Fifth Ward Missionary Baptist, replied. "He kept saying he cares about the people—'I don't want anyone to be heartbroken!' Yet we're not seeing much action on his part. I think he needed to hear our stories to get a better picture of what people are dealing with. The story you shared with him about Lena was perfect; it's too bad she was too ill to tell it herself."

"I hope it got our point across, that people are confused and don't know what to do. The city really needs to be more involved in helping people," Ruby said. "I hope our meeting today can clear some things up with the mayor, and that our relationship hasn't been damaged too much."

Several minutes later Mayor Turner opened his office door.

"Hello, everyone. Come on in," he said.

The women walked into his office and saw there was another guest present.

"This is Tom, the Housing and Development Coordinator," Mayor Turner said. "I've asked him to join us today. I've got something I'd like to share with all of you about an encounter I had recently."

Sheyda, Paula, Ruby, and the others sat up straight, curious to hear what he had to say.

"So, last week I was on my lunch break and decided to go to Whataburger. While I was in the drive-through, the cashier recognized me as the mayor and told me about his mom, who had not yet received any help on her house. I told the man to write down her information and that I would pass it on to our Housing and Development Coordinator." He paused and looked at Tom. "So, Tom, here you go!" he said, handing him a piece of paper. "I'd like for you to contact this woman today and see what we can do to get some repairs going on her house."

Tom took the paper. "Yes sir! I will give her a call this afternoon."

"So," said Mayor Turner, looking at Sheyda and Paula, "I wanted to share this with you to let you know that I'm going to be doing more to get people the help they need."

Ruby and Sheyda gave each other a side glance. *So, is that what it takes for people to get help from the city?!* Sheyda thought. *They need to have a personal connection or encounter with the mayor himself?!*

References

City of Houston Planning and Development Department (2017a, November). Super neighborhood resource assessment. Greater third ward. Retrieved June 6, 2018, from www.houstontx.gov/planning/Demographics/docs_pdfs/SN/67_Greater_ThirdWar.pdf

City of Houston Planning and Development Department (2017b, November). Super neighborhood resource assessment. Greater fifth ward. Retrieved June 6,

2018, from www.houstontx.gov/planning/Demographics/docs_pdfs/SN/67_ Greater_FifthWard.pdf

U.S. Census Bureau (2016). ACS demographic and housing estimates, 2012–2016 American Community Survey 5 Year Estimates. Retrieved from https://factfinder. census.gov/faces/tableservices/jsf/pages/productview.xhtml?pid=ACS_16_5YR_ DP05&prodType=table

Wright, L. (2018, January). The glut economy. *The New Yorker*, 42–53.

Part IV

Experienced MSW Practitioners

12 Ascension

The Board Meeting

Several months into her job, Angela sat in her car in the parking lot and thought about the meeting she was about to enter. *I'm not having fun*, she thought. *These meetings are the part I like least about my job. Every decision I make just ticks people off. I'm trying to make changes I feel are important, that will help fulfill the agency's mission, yet I don't feel very supported. Last week I asked everyone why they served on the board, and not one person mentioned the mission. This is just a social hour for them. How can I get anything done when I'm not sure anyone really cares about what we're trying to do?* She took a deep breath and opened her door. *Oh, I hope this meeting will go well*, she thought as she stepped out and made her way to the office.

Angela Jefferson

Angela Jefferson was born and raised in Chicago. She earned her MSW from the University of Illinois Jane Addams College of Social Work, where she met her husband, Anthony. The two soon moved to Kansas City to begin their careers and a family. Angela started working as a caseworker at a local homeless shelter and soon moved into an administrative position, eventually becoming the executive director.

After 15 years she began considering a career change. She told Anthony, "You know I've always used ascending stairs as my barometer for work satisfaction; sure, I'm getting older, but I just don't ascend the way I used to. I've done *a lot* for this agency like a successful capital campaign and expanded sites and services. But I'm not happy about the way the city wants to use the new grant I got for the shelter, and it just seems like it's time to try something new. I think I'm going to start looking around for a new job."

Soon thereafter, she heard the executive director for Methodist Urban Ministry (MUM), Betty Lewis, was leaving, and Angela looked at their website. She was intrigued that part of the agency's mission was to "eliminate racism." She decided to call Betty about the position. At the end of a very long conversation Betty told Angela, "I think you'd be perfect for the job. There is an internal candidate, but I think you'd be a better choice. Please apply!"

Over dinner that night, Angela told Anthony about the conversation. "I'm seriously thinking of applying. What do you think?"

"I think it's great! After all the racism we've experienced in our personal lives and your passion for social justice, I think you'd be perfect for the job, too. Are there any other people of color at the agency or on the board?"

"The board is all white, and none of the program directors are black or Hispanic. So that might be something for me to start working on right away."

Angela applied for the job, was interviewed by the board, and offered the position on the spot. Immediately after, Angela called her husband, excited about the news. "They offered, and I accepted! I think a few of them were nervous about my excitement around eliminating racism—they seemed leery, but they didn't know how to say no. So, there are probably going to be a few uphill battles, but that's ok."

Methodist Urban Ministry (MUM)

Founded in 1969, MUM worked to provide support to multicultural communities through programs that included counseling services, a small food pantry, and immigrant/refugee services. Since its inception, MUM had continually evolved to meet the needs of families and the community of Kansas City. At its peak, the agency served over 20,000 people through programs offered at two separate locations. At its core, the mission of the agency focused on empowering families and minorities, promoting social justice, and eliminating racism.

MUM was funded primarily by private donations, including the Missouri Conference of the United Methodist Church and the United Way. The counseling service fees generated income, but not enough to cover the costs. The agency also relied heavily on volunteers to assist with the day-to-day agency operations, and fundraising and development.

The Organizational Chart

The MUM board consisted of 28 members, many of whom had been on the board for 18–23 years. The policy allowed members to serve for six years at a time. Many members would take a gap year and resume membership the following year. All the board members were white women, and many of them were older, wealthy professionals.

MUM also had a CEO and a CFO, followed by Angela as the executive director and four program directors. A social justice director oversaw the implementation of the agency's mission. MUM employed several other employees beneath these directors to help run the programs and services. All directors hired their own employees and set their salaries. The management team had 22 employees, including various coordinators that oversaw English as a Second Language classes, refugee and immigration services, and various food donation programs. The executive director, CFO, CEO, and program directors met weekly and the coordinators met monthly.

Lunch with the Board President: "This Really is Working Fine"

Two weeks before starting her position as the new executive director for the MUM, Cindy, the board president, invited Angela to an informal lunch at Capital Grill. Prior to the meeting, Angela had received several documents from Cindy. While looking over the organizational chart, Angela had noticed something surprising and decided to bring it up.

"Cindy, I was looking over the organizational chart you gave me and I saw two last names that are the same. Is this a coincidence, or are Bob and Mary Gallagher related?" Angela asked.

"Yes, they are father and daughter" Cindy said, after she swallowed a bite of her lobster salad. "As a matter of fact, Mary reports to Bob."

Angela raised her eyebrows. "Hmm, I was wondering whether that was the case. I think I might have to change that."

Cindy shifted in her seat. "No, no, this really is working fine," she stated. "It has been going on longer than we anticipated, but it's working."

"Could you tell me why this happened and how it started?" Angela inquired.

"Well, Mary graduated from college and after eight months still could not find a job. There was a half-time position opening and the board thought she could fill the position while she continued to look for work." She paused. "I can't really tell you when it turned into a full-time position, but it seemed to be working so we just let her stay."

This doesn't seem right, thought Angela.

Cindy continued, "We're like a family, and we operate like a family, so I think it works fine. Nobody has any problems with it."

Angela left the lunch meeting shaking her head. *That just seems like a problem to me*, she thought. *I can't understand why no one else at this organization sees it that way, too.*

★★★

The following day Angela received a call from Cindy.

"Hi Angela, it's Cindy. I just wanted to let you know that I spoke with Betty about the concern you raised. She's going to have Mary start reporting to her instead of her father. She thought you had a point and it seemed like the appropriate thing to do."

Well that's good! thought Angela, relieved at having one less issue to tackle when she started her job.

First Day on the Job

Angela ran up the steps and into her office at MUM feeling excited about her role as the new executive director and ready to get started. She sat down at her desk and started up her computer. While she waited for her email to open Cindy walked in.

"Hi, Angela! Welcome to your first day on the job! Are you ready to get started?"

"Hi Cindy. Yes, I am very excited to be here!" Angela replied.

"Great!" said Cindy. "Hey, I wanted to give you an updated copy of our organizational chart." Cindy placed some papers on Angela's desk.

"Thank you." Angela started scanning it over. "That's interesting, I don't see Mary's name on here."

"Oh," said Cindy, "we let her go last week." She paused, then said, "When she started reporting to the former executive director, Betty discovered she wasn't a very productive worker. Turns out Bob did a lot of Mary's workload for her and this upset the other employees." As she headed for the door she added, "It didn't make sense to pay two people for work that could be done by one person."

"It's Going to End"

In July, a few weeks after she was hired, Angela learned that family members working together at MUM was not uncommon. She discovered that one staff member on the administrative team worked with her mother. Additionally, the children of two other employees on the management team worked at MUM over the summer, which turned out to be a common practice. She hadn't caught this on the organizational chart because they had different last names.

As Angela looked over the personnel policies, she noticed family members were not just allowed but encouraged to work within the agency. As for reporting relationships, there was nothing that prohibited family members from reporting to each other, but approval was required by the executive director.

During a management team meeting, Angela brought up her findings.

"After looking over the policies, I understand why family members are working here," she said, "but it's going to end. So, I'm going to be revising the policy, working with the HR committee, and I don't want anyone hiring any more family members until that happens."

Lisa Adams, the CFO, spoke up. "Could we readdress this policy in August? My daughter just started and planned on working here through the summer."

Oh great, Angela thought as she processed the request. *I'm making some big changes here. Does it matter if I make the change now or in a month? Either way, I'm going to be the "bad guy."*

"OK, sure," Angela said. "We can wait until August. But no more hiring family members. I'll put out a memo in the meantime to let everyone know I'm working on a new policy."

As Angela began to better understand the agency, its functions, and dynamics, she discovered some other practices that she found disturbing. *There seems to be very little supervision here, and a lot of leeway in each program. Like, although the counseling services are generating revenue, the counselors don't appear to be using best-practices. The counselors are all masters-level and licensed, but they have their clients that they really like, and they have groups that they are doing that they really like, and that seems to be driving the interventions, not best-practices. There's one client who's been in therapy for five years!*

The Board Meeting

Several months into her job, Angela sat in her car in the parking lot and thought about the meeting she was about to enter. *I'm not having fun,* she thought. *These meetings are the part I like least about my job. Every decision I make just ticks people off. I'm trying to make changes I feel are important, that will help fulfill the agency's mission, especially around combatting racism, yet I don't feel very supported. Last week I asked everyone why they served on the board, and not one person mentioned the mission or eliminating racism. It was all about "relationships" and "friendships" and "the empowerment we experience from being on an all-female board and raising money." This is just a social hour for them. How can I get anything done when I'm not sure anyone really cares about what we're trying to do?* She took a deep breath and opened her door. *Oh, I hope this meeting will go well,* she thought as she stepped out and made her way to the office.

★★★

Angela entered the meeting room and spread out her papers at the head of the long table. She read over her agenda for the day, running through the points she wanted to cover. Board members began filing in and her stomach tightened.

"Good morning everyone," she started. "Thank you for being here today. I wanted to revisit our mission statement and talk a bit about how we are fulfilling it. Let's start with 'eliminating racism.' What are your thoughts?"

After sipping her Pellegrino, Dierdre Hall spoke up. "I think we've met our mission of eliminating racism by providing services in mid-town, east of Troost Avenue."

Angela's stomach tightened more. *Is that all it takes?* she thought, hoping her face looked neutral. *This is going to be a long meeting . . .*

13 I Want to Hold My Babies!

"I think she needs to see all the kids, not just the older ones!" Elena pleaded to her clinical director, Carissa. "I mean, everything I know about infant mental health indicates disrupting attachment with their mom could be devastating to those kids."

"What are you wanting to do though, Elena?" Carissa asked patiently. "I guess you could rattle some cages and advocate, but they are the experts in child protective services and they make the decisions."

"But weeks and weeks have already gone by. She needs to see those kids," Elena protested.

"At the end of the day, Elena," Carissa responded, "we all have to do our jobs. Their job is to protect the kids, and your job is to help Veronica recover from addiction. This is outside of your purview, outside of your job description. Maybe *you* need to focus on her recovery just like *she* needs to focus on her recovery."

From San Antonio to Laredo

Beautiful San Antonio, Texas was the home to more than a million people, more than half of whom were Hispanic or Latino/a of any race. Steeped in Texas culture and the influence of Mexico, San Antonio was popular for tourism, especially in the Riverwalk area and at the Alamo. The city also was home to Six Flags Fiesta Texas and the controversial SeaWorld.

About 150 miles south was the city of Laredo, almost 95% Hispanic or Latino/a, just north of the Rio Grande. Laredo's mix of Spanish Colonial architecture and Mexican inspired buildings made it a city that was attractive for more than just its position as a trade port and a border crossing point. The Immigration Border Patrol was a major employer. The city itself had a poverty rate of more than 30%, and a significant pay gap for women, who averaged only $24,700 annually compared to $35,000 for men.

Between Laredo and San Antonio was the Rio Grande Plain, part prairie, and part brush of prickly pear, small oaks, and cacti. The area was good for raising livestock, mostly cattle, sheep, and goats. Irrigation allowed some vegetable farming, but the land was mostly hot and dry.

La Vida Alegre

As a residential substance abuse facility, the staff at La Vida Alegre had a philosophy that treating the whole person in a setting that incorporated nature, spirituality, and evidence-based therapy practices could help create a meaningful recovery from substance abuse disorders. Located on 40 sprawling acres just north of the Rio Grande, about an hour down Interstate 35 towards Laredo from San Antonio, the land was more fertile than the rest of the prairie and contained a small grove of orange trees. The staff at La Vida Alegre could treat up to 20 men and 18 women in the residential facilities, for 30, 60, or 90 days, but usually kept the numbers smaller due to open staff positions and to improve the staff to client ratio.

Funding for the agency was through the state, based on qualifications determined by the ASAM (American Society for Addiction Medicine) criteria at intake. Many clients were court ordered, either seeking treatment to avoid criminal charges, or ordered as part of a child protective services reunification plan. But some were voluntary, seeking intensive treatment. The majority of the clients abused opioids, mostly heroin, but methamphetamine and alcohol were also common drugs of choice.

Enjoying the rugged beauty of the land, the staff kept chickens, several sheep, horses, a small herd of goats, and two blue heeler dogs on the property. The residents helped staff care for the animals, and also grew corn, spinach, peppers, and tomatoes in the garden areas. The produce and eggs were used in the cafeteria and occasionally sold at a roadside farm stand, with the proceeds funding further care of the animals and plants.

The agency was directed by the CEO, Eduardo deVilla, a Licensed Clinical Social Worker (LCSW) in his 50s, who was born and raised in Laredo by parents who immigrated from Mexico. He was passionate about holistic treatment, treating employees and clients with respect, and valuing self-care. He was willing to make arrangements for a day off, leaves of absences and part-time work schedules when needed and arranging coverage for staff who needed extra time to catch up with paperwork or spend extra time serving a client. The clinical staff was supervised by the Clinical Director, Carissa Castille, LCSW, who was in her early 40s and had been with La Vida Alegre for more than 12 years. Carissa was also a Texas native raised by immigrant parents from Mexico. She had a reputation of being organized, empathetic, and also very devoted to holistic treatment for addiction.

Services at the agency included a recreational therapist who utilized the softball field, volleyball court, basketball court, and gym equipment to promote exercise. There was a yoga instructor, as well as spiritual leaders of different denominations and cultural backgrounds to provide culturally competent spiritual guidance. Treatment was gender specific; men and women were treated separately, instructed not to look at each other, talk to each other, or interact in any way. Residents were required to attend three therapeutic groups a day, each facilitated by a licensed clinician. One group leader used the curriculum "Living in Balance," another utilized "Seeking

Safety," and a third clinician focused on emotion identification, emotion regulation, and relationship dynamics. In the evenings, attendants provided groups, including 12-step groups like Alcoholics Anonymous and Narcotics Anonymous, but also general peer support discussions, educational groups about substances and recovery, and the recreational opportunities.

The staff of La Vida Alegre conducted random urine analysis testing, and if a client tested positive for substances, discharge was immediate. But even with the immediate discharge, the client met with the case manager for an aftercare plan and the other residents were called together to say goodbye. This included tears and hugs as the residents and staff expressed genuine wishes for the client's recovery and created a positive sendoff.

Elena Glass

Elena Glass was an experienced social worker, having worked with her MSW and license for more than 30 years. As an attractive, Caucasian, divorced woman in her early 60s, she had recently moved to San Antonio from her home in Nebraska hoping for new adventures and a new start in life. While her social work experience in Nebraska ranged from working in hospice, working with elementary and middle school age children, teaching at the University of Nebraska, and operating a private practice for children and families, she had never before worked in the field of substance abuse. While she had confronted issues of substance abuse with her children she raised as a single mother, and had encountered substance abuse among families, it had never been a focus of practice. She was excited to learn more and develop her skills.

Living alone in Texas was enjoyable for Elena, who loved taking long walks with her dog, gardening, and making new friends. She loved the art museums and the energy of San Antonio, but also liked to get out of town to hike and explore. She liked working hard, including teaching a class in family development as an adjunct instructor at Texas A&M's San Antonio campus, taking advantage of her PhD in Family and Child Development she had earned about 15 years previously when her children were young.

Elena provided a therapy group at La Vida Alegre on impulse control for adults, realizing that poor impulse control was part of the picture in substance abuse, a risk factor for substance abuse with children, and a reason many residents left treatment sooner than recommended. She had developed a practice specialty in impulse control with children and felt the cognitive and behavioral skills could easily be extrapolated to work with adults and substance abuse. She also provided a living skills group that included money management, health and safety, and other daily life skills that some clients needed to develop if they were to succeed working and living on their own without substances.

Like all the therapists, Elena also had a caseload of individual clients. She had noticed she provided more family therapy than other clinicians, often inviting spouses or family members to attend sessions. Her colleagues had commented on this before, some mentioning it was important for the client to work on themselves in residential treatment, away from the burdens of their usual lives, building their own strength in recovery before tackling family issues. But Elena believed in supporting relationships, not wanting to separate clients from their loved ones and the complexities of family life, and helping families recover together.

Veronica Lopez, Mother of Ten

Elena sat quietly at her desk, writing case notes by hand, when Carissa appeared in her doorway.

"Elena," Carissa began. "You know Veronica, who was admitted a couple weeks ago?"

"Yeah," Elena responded. "The one whose husband is here too and keeps yelling 'I love you' across the fence at her?"

"That's the one!" Carissa smiled. "Not sure admitting a couple together was such a great idea. But anyway, I'd like you to see her for individual therapy. She was seeing Darlene, and that was fine, but I really think she needs to see one of the full-time therapists. Darlene is cutting her hours back to just two days a week and I want this client to have more consistency than that."

"Sure," Elena answered. "No problem. Is she here now for me to meet with her?"

"Yes," Carissa responded. "Darlene told her she would get someone new, and she was ok with it. But she's out working in the garden if you wanted to go grab her and say hello."

"OK, I'll go get her," Elena said, rising from her chair. She walked outside and made her way to the garden where three women were pulling weeds around tomato plants.

"Veronica?" Elena asked a small, thin, well-groomed woman with long, straight dark hair. The woman raised her head and smiled.

"Are you my new therapist?" she asked.

"Yep," Elena answered. "How about if we go ahead and meet?"

Veronica and Elena walked back to the administrative building and settled in Elena's office.

"So, I know you were meeting with Darlene," Elena began. "But catch me up, I'm just jumping in."

"Well I'm here because of alcohol, it's a real problem for me," Veronica admitted. "CPS took all my kids after they came to our house in San Antonio and said it wasn't ok to not have electricity and water. They said things were real bad and they took them all."

"Tell me about your children," Elena prompted.

"Ok, there's Luis who's 14, and his dad is out in Brownsville. Juan's 11, and Mario's 9, and their dad used to be abusive, but not as bad as the next one. I had Julia who's 8 now and Guille's 7, but their dad used to lock me up in a room and beat me, and just leave the babies crying in the other room and I couldn't get to them. But I left him and ended up with Javier. We have

Samuel who's 5, Ana's 4, Maria's 2 now and the twins, Daniel and Gabriel, are 18 months. They told me the babies were real delayed because they aren't really talking yet, but I know several of my boys were late talkers."

"So what happened after the kids were gone?" Elena asked.

"I went berserk," Veronica said frankly. "They were all spread out in different foster homes, and I just started drinking and stayed drunk 24/7. Went on for months like that, just drinking, and feeling sorry for myself, and fighting with Javier. And I didn't do the visitation. The caseworker said I could, but I was just too drunk and messed up to deal with it. But one day I woke up and said to myself 'this is not where I want to go, I want my children back.' So I went down to the CPS office to get visitation all lined up, and they told me about this place. I've never done any treatment before, so I thought I'd give it a try if it will help me get my babies back."

"I'm impressed," Elena said supportively. "Most people have been in treatment several times before they come here, and I'm glad you are just making the decision to do this for yourself and your family."

"I really want my kids back," Veronica said emphatically. "I miss them."

"I can tell," Elena responded. "So, tell me about a time when your life was stable?" This standard question was on the psychosocial assessment form and was one that Elena found often revealed some strengths.

"Three years ago," Veronica answered. "I had the kids of course, we were living in Corpus Christi then because Javier had a job in construction. But that job ended and we ended up back in San Antonio and that's when we started fighting so much and drinking more. And he started in on meth."

"Sounds like you really felt like you could take care of the kids well when you were in Corpus Christi," Elena reflected.

"I could. Everyone was there and we were doing good."

Elena was quiet and noticed tears welling in Veronica's eyes.

"I've been drinking a long time," she said sadly. "Started when my dad died. He was a good guy and he passed when I was about 14. Emphysema."

Elena nodded attentively and allowed for silence until Veronica continued.

"Anyway, it was also the same year as the rape. Nine boys." Veronica looked away but continued to speak. "Never prosecuted, police didn't care. No one listens to a little Mexican girl talking about the boys in the town doing something wrong. But there you go, 14 years old and drinking."

Nine boys? Elena thought angrily. *That's a horrific gang rape. She seems to minimize it, but I am sure she has numerous difficulties as a result of a trauma like that. And right as she lost her dad?*

The session continued, including Veronica mentioning difficulty falling asleep at night, often awake for four to five hours, and early awakening at three or four in the morning. After Veronica left, Elena wrote her note. *CPS involvement due to alcoholism, client takes responsibility for use of alcohol and effects on children,* Elena wrote. *She identified her traumas and her anxiety, including having difficulty sleeping. Discussed seeing psychiatric nurse for medication evaluation.*

Difficulty Sleeping

A few days later, Elena received a call from Yolanda Carter, RN, the psychiatric nurse for the agency.

"So I'm told you are trying to get a bunch of sleeping meds for Veronica," the nurse began.

"She is having great difficulty sleeping," Elena explained.

"Well, she doesn't need a bunch of drugs", the nurse said brusquely. "She can't sleep because she's withdrawing! Don't you know that? She doesn't need anything, she'll sleep in a couple of weeks."

"She will not be able to focus on treatment if she is tired and not sleeping," Elena pushed. "She needs medication." *Why do I have to go through Nurse Ratched to get my clients some help?* Elena thought.

"It's part of the process of withdrawing," the nurse retorted. "She has to go through it like everyone else. Maybe you're just being snowed."

"I have diagnosed this client with an anxiety disorder and PTSD, and I need her to be thoroughly evaluated for medications to alleviate her symptoms," Elena said firmly. *I know as a clinician, I tend to see the positive,* Elena thought. *It's a good, strengths perspective and I wouldn't change it, but I know I might err in missing subtle alerts that may be negative. But that doesn't mean this client doesn't need help sleeping.*

"I can see what I can do," the nurse said unconvincingly.

Field Trip

By the following week, Veronica had medication to help her sleep, and seemed more alert and rested. But the staff had been troubled by the interactions between her and her husband.

"Veronica, I heard what happened yesterday evening during the recreation switch. Are you ok?" Elena asked at their session.

"You mean with Javier?" Veronica asked. "Meh, he's just like that."

"Tell me what happened then, so I hear it from you."

"Oh, during the time when the men go inside and the women go out to the rec field, he always shouts at me over the fence," she began. At first it was all, 'Veronica, I love you!' and 'I miss you so much!' But I guess he found out about those two new girls on the unit now."

"Stephanie and Kate?" Elena asked.

"Yeah, the lesbians," Veronica replied. "So he was like, 'Veronica, you better not be screwing around with those dykes! Are you having sex with them, bitch?'"

"Wow," Elena responded simply, not sure what to say. "What was that like for you?"

"He's just full of shit. He just doesn't like it when he doesn't know what I'm doing. Back home, I rarely left the house, so he didn't worry so much."

"Was that because you feared him or because of your own anxiety?" Elena wondered. "Or maybe it was all the same thing?"

"I don't know, but I would get too nervous to even go to the grocery store," Veronica disclosed.

"So what did you do when you needed something?" Elena asked.

"If my husband couldn't get it, I'd send one of the older kids," Veronica responded. "But I haven't had a job in years. I can't even imagine that, leaving the house every day."

"Let's take a field trip," Elena said with a grin. She called the facilities manager to let him know she was taking a client off campus, signed the check-out sheet, and led Veronica to her car. She then drove Veronica to the convenience store a few blocks away.

"Go in and buy some candy," she said, handing Veronica two $1 bills. "Use the relaxation techniques we have used. I'll follow you just in case you need help."

Veronica looked nervous but opened the car door and walked inside. She stopped at the front door and took deep breaths.

"How high is your anxiety right now, on a scale of 1 to 10 with 1 is no anxiety at all and 10 is through the roof panic?" Elena asked.

"Growing," Veronica answered. "Maybe a 7?"

"So what are you going to do to manage that?" Elena prompted. She could tell Veronica was still breathing deeply and was clinching and relaxing her hands. She had her eyes closed.

"Ok, a 4," Veronica said after a couple of minutes, putting her hand on the door and walking in. She continued to speak aloud about her anxiety and coping skills as she successfully chose a candy bar, paid for it, gave Elena the change, and returned to the car.

"You did it," Elena praised.

"I did the breathing, and then repeated that phrase over and over again whenever my brain started freaking out," Veronica said proudly.

"What phrase?" Elena asked.

"You won't die," Veronica said smiling. "No one died from buying candy. At least I don't think so."

"Not on my watch," Elena said, laughing.

"I didn't realize that if you just keep doing it over and over," Veronica began, "practicing the things you said might help, eventually it gets better."

"I'm proud of you, Veronica," Elena praised again. "Where's your anxiety at now on the scale?"

"Pretty low," Veronica answered. "Like a 2."

"That's pretty good," Elena said, smiling. "Any lower and you might fall asleep."

Veronica smiled.

"I bought Juan's favorite, peanut butter cups," Veronica said. "I'll save it for when I am done here and get to start visitation again."

"But you had started visitation before you came here, right? Why did it stop?" Elena asked, driving through the gate of La Vida Alegre.

"Well, I can't leave here. And we were having visitation at the CPS office." Veronica said, giving Elena a quizzical look.

"Well, can't they bring them here?" Elena asked. "I mean, I have other clients who have visitation with their kids. The worker drives them here and they can play with them outside or in the game room." *Bless her heart*, Elena thought. *She is just ignorant of the system and didn't think to ask.*

"I didn't know that!" Veronica exclaimed, her face lighting up. "I never thought of that!"

"I'll call your case worker," Elena offered as Veronica left for the residence hall.

"Elena!" called the facilities manager, Alberto, as Elena was walking back towards her office. She stepped back to stand in his open doorway.

"Elena," Alberto said. "Did you drive Veronica somewhere?"

"Yes, I told you that," Elena said. "Remember, I said we were going to the convenience store and we signed out."

"But in your own car?" Alberto asked. "You have to take the company van. Big problem with your own car."

"Oh, sorry, I didn't know that," Elena explained. Carissa had now stepped into the hallway as well.

"Just be sure and use the van," Carissa interjected. "But why did you do that anyway? You don't need to be driving folks around just because they want some soda or whatever. They are supposed to stay on campus. You can't let them talk you into stuff like that."

"It was in vivo treatment for anxiety," Elena explained. "For her to practice anxiety management techniques in a real-life setting."

"Oh, ok, I see, that's fine," Carissa said. "Just not in your car, ok?"

The Infant Mental Health Consultant

"How was the visit with the kiddos?" Elena asked a couple sessions later. Elena knew visitation had started to occur after she called the caseworker.

"So good," Veronica said, smiling. "They are doing well in school and they liked playing horseshoes out on the lawn. It was a good time. The worker will bring them back next week. But I wish I could see the little ones too."

"What do you mean?" Elena asked. "Weren't they all there?"

"No, not the babies," Veronica answered. "Just the older five."

"What's that about?" Elena wondered aloud. "Why did they say they just brought five of them?"

"The worker just said that is how it was. Just the older five could come."

"Veronica, that's not right, it couldn't be," Elena said. "I'll try to figure this out."

After Veronica left the session, Elena called the CPS worker for Veronica's case.

"Good morning," Elena said pleasantly, "I spoke to you a couple weeks ago about Veronica Lopez and visitation with her kids out here at La Vida Alegre."

"Yes," answered Jessica Pritchett, the CPS worker, "I remember. We brought the kids out there."

"Right, and that's great, thank you," Elena said. "But what about the five little ones? The five older ones visited, but not the little ones?"

"Oh, the little ones fall under the infant mental health protocols," explained Jessica. "That's for any kids under six."

"So what does that mean?" Elena asked.

"Well, we have an infant mental health consultant," Jessica said, "and the little kids have an assessment and treatment plan from her, not from us. So it's a separate thing, up to her. She didn't think they should visit right now."

"I'd like to speak to her, could I have her contact information?" Elena asked.

"Ok," Jessica said with a slight hesitation. "I think that is OK." She gave the contact information for Lillian Verdad, a licensed counselor and certified infant mental health specialist.

"Good morning," Elena said when Lillian answered, "I'm Elena Glass and I'm the therapist for Veronica Lopez. I wanted to talk to you about setting up visitation for her youngest five children here at La Vida Alegre. I just talked to Jessica at the CPS office and she gave me your information."

"Yes, I've worked with those children," Lillian responded. "I do not think it is a good idea to bring them to see her at your facility."

"Oh, we have lots of great visitation spaces here," Elena responded. "Several of my clients have their kids come visit. And I know Veronica's older ones have done well visiting and would love to see their siblings."

"These are children who have experienced trauma," Lillian said. "They need an atmosphere of routine and stability, and it might be upsetting to them to be at a drug and alcohol treatment facility."

"I understand they have experienced trauma, but they need to see their mother, especially if reunification is the plan, don't they?" Elena asked.

"It would be disruptive to their routines, potentially retraumatizing, and might impair their progress to drive such a distance and be in that environment," Lillian stated.

"It's just an hour," Elena countered. "We aren't all the way to Laredo, but just outside of Pearsall. And I have read a great deal about infant mental health. My understanding is that the children need to spend time with the parent to not further disrupt attachment. If indeed the parent is working their plan and there is going to be reunification. There needs to be attachment."

"These children are severely delayed, have been exposed to domestic violence, and to substance abuse," Lillian stated. "It is our position that it is not in their best interests to have visitation at this time at the facility. Thank you for your concern, and please have Ms. Lopez contact our office when she has completed treatment and can resume visits at the CPS office."

This is Not Fair!

Veronica was tearful when she arrived for her next session, looking like she had been crying for a long time.

"What's wrong?" Elena asked.

"It's Luis, my oldest," Veronica said sadly. "He called me and said that he wants to go live with his father. In Brownsville."

"Oh, Veronica," Elena empathized. "I know you will really miss him."

"He's the artist of the family, I have some of his drawings with me," Veronica shared. "I know he's not happy where he's at. I don't know if he'll be happy with his father, but he deserves a chance to find out."

"You can still see him though, right?" Elena asked. "Visitation?"

"The CPS worker said I will still have my parental rights," Veronica said. "But I'm turning over custody, so it is up to his father as to if I see him. I don't know. But he is coming here one last time on Thursday to say good-bye. He's a sensitive boy, I know he'll be sad too. And he is so close with Juan and Mario, they'll miss each other."

"Well, I am sorry you have to go through this," Elena said. *She really seems to know all these kids, even though there are ten of them,* Elena thought.

"What did you find out about my babies?" Veronica asked, hopefully.

Elena explained the situation with the infant mental health specialist and the concerns about visitation.

"Are you kidding me?" Veronica said, her voice rising. "Who is this lady? Who does she think she is deciding I can't see my own babies?"

"Well, I know you are angry, but let's stop and think a second about how to address this," Elena said.

"Oh, I'll address it," Veronica said emphatically. "Give me her name and number and I'll call her right now. I will tell her exactly what I think of her."

"Wait though, Veronica," Elena said calmly. "Remember about stopping and thinking when you are angry? Do you want to be reactive and cuss her out or do you want to sleep on it and we can work on writing a letter?"

"No letter from me is going to do any good," Veronica said.

"It might. But regardless, which reaction makes you look like a competent parent?" Elena asked. "That's what you want them to see, right?"

Veronica's face softened and she became tearful again and slumped in her chair.

"I just want to hold my babies," she finally said through tears. "I just want to hold them."

Seeking Help from Carissa

After the sad session with Veronica, Elena looked for Carissa to staff the case.

"I think she needs to see all the kids, not just the older ones!" Elena pleaded to Carissa. "I mean, everything I know about infant mental health indicates disrupting attachment with their mom could be devastating to those kids."

"What are you wanting to do though, Elena?" Carissa asked patiently. "I guess you could rattle some cages and advocate, but they are the experts in child protective services and they make the decisions."

"But weeks and weeks have already gone by. She needs to see those kids," Elena protested.

"At the end of the day, Elena," Carissa responded, "we all have to do our jobs. Their job is to protect the kids, and your job is to help Veronica recover from addiction. This is outside of your purview, outside of your job description. Maybe *you* need to focus on her recovery just like *she* needs to focus on her recovery."

But how can she focus on her recovery if she is being kept away from her family, worrying about them and missing them? Elena thought. *I want to advocate for her, but don't know where to begin. Or if it is worth it to fight this fight. But she might be here another 60 days and that is a lifetime for those little children. What is the best way to help Veronica?*

14 Call Me Cam

Kathryn Chase closed the door gently behind Abby and Cam Murphy as they left her office. She sat down in her comfortable striped wingchair to think a moment about what had just occurred. *Cam deserves to have what he needs to be himself, but I don't feel right about the differences in how he and Abby describe Cam's level of support at home. And well, this is a pretty young kid and there is a part of me that worries about injecting large doses of testosterone into a vulnerable teenager.*

Welcome to Football Country

The city of Fort Worth, Texas, promoting itself as the "City of Cowboys and Culture," was known for its attractions related to western heritage, rodeos, country music, and longhorn cattle, but also for its respectable museums of modern and American art, the art-deco style of the bustling downtown, and as the host of the prestigious Van Cliburn International Piano Competition. While it was difficult at points to tell where Fort Worth ended and Dallas began, making travel sometimes longer than expected, Fort Worth residents saw their city as distinct from the urban environment of Dallas.

The Texas Motor Speedway was a major tourist attraction to see NASCAR racing and IndyCars. The Texas Rangers played baseball in nearby Arlington. The sunny climate made Fort Worth popular for golf, running, biking, and all kinds of outdoor recreation. But on football game days, practically the whole city dressed in purple for the Texas Christian University Horned Frogs. The TCU team was part of the Big 12 Conference of college football, and if one preferred professional football, the Dallas Cowboys played nearby. The culture of sports, particularly football, started early and most of the boys in the Fort Worth public schools were involved in at least one competitive sport.

Bathroom Backlash

The Fort Worth public schools had policies in place to protect children from discrimination or bullying due to sexual orientation, gender identity, or perceived sexual orientation. But like much of the U.S. in 2017, the schools struggled with the issue of transgender kids and bathrooms. While the Obama Administration supported transgender students' identities being respected in schools in 2016, Fort Worth amended their policy to require parental consent and a parent initiated request before allowing bathroom choices for trans-youth. But soon 36 states were proposing "bathroom bills" attempting to limit transgender rights. By February of 2017, the newly elected President had rescinded protection for transgender students to use bathrooms corresponding to gender identity. Many transgender students were left feeling uncomfortable and unsafe in either bathroom and many avoided using them altogether.

Kathryn Chase, LCSW

Kathryn Chase was a white woman with curly blond hair with a thriving private practice. While she had experience with community mental health and public health, she had joined with a colleague in 2014 to rent office space in the northern part of Fort Worth and form a private practice. Her colleague left the practice, so she found another office very close to her home. It was spacious and comfortable, and worked well for her very diverse clients.

As a fluent Spanish speaker, she had several clients and families that preferred their sessions in Spanish. Many of these clients were migrants and had settled in Texas. She saw several clients that were gay or lesbian and had worked with transgender adults and youth before. She had also worked with family members of transgender clients to help them understand how to support their loved one through often difficult times.

Kathryn herself was raised in Texas but had lived in several other states including North Carolina where she received her MSW in 1999. She and her husband had returned to Texas to be closer to her mother and were happy living in familiar Fort Worth with their three German Shepherds.

Evaluation Request

Kathryn had just hung up her coat and purse at her private practice office when the phone rang.

"I was wondering if you do HRT evaluations," asked the caller.

"Hormone Replacement Therapy?" Kathryn asked. "Well, I want to clarify that I do therapy, not just quick evaluations. So, while I have written letters about this type of thing before, it has been as a part of ongoing treatment due to depression, anxiety, family stress, or something like that. But can you tell me more about what you need?"

The caller introduced herself as Abby Murphy and began to relate the story.

"I'm calling about my … child … Camilla," Abby began. "She's 15, and you know, has been, uh, dressing as a boy and living as a boy for the past year and we have been really supportive of that because we want him to be comfortable."

"But things have started to kind of fall apart," Abby continued. "Camilla seems so anxious about social situations and going to school this year. He has like, psychosomatic stomach distress. Like coming in saying he's too sick for school because of diarrhea. And I know it is psychosomatic because she has gone to the doctor and we got everything checked out. She keeps saying she wants to start the hormones, but this doctor won't do it."

"Right," Kathryn agreed. She had known some people who had good luck at Planned Parenthood, but a run of the mill gynecologist or family doctor usually wouldn't have the familiarity or would have some kind of opposition to it. Plus, there were several steps before treatment could begin.

"I just, I mean, we want to be supportive," Abby continued. "But I guess I don't know what to do right now."

"It sounds like they have a lot of anxiety," Kathryn began. "We could definitely talk about that. There is a lot of symptom management that can happen here that can maybe make their life a little more comfortable."

Kathryn arranged a meeting for the following week to meet the family.

Meeting Cam and Abby

Kathryn smiled at the family in the waiting room, introduced herself, and led them back to her office. *If I had seen this kiddo walking on the street, I would have assumed he was a boy*, she thought. *Sort of an effeminate boy, without a masculine-sounding voice, but certainly a boy.*

"I like to see parents and kids together first, to discuss confidentiality, and what I have to share with your mom," Kathryn said. She looked at the child, who stared at the floor. "But first," she said brightly, "what name would you like for me to call you? And what pronouns do you prefer?"

"Cam. And he," he said. Cam looked at her through his brown hair, longish on the top, that flopped over in his eyes. He had a slight frame, tight black jeans, and a baggy black t-shirt. *In my day, we would have called him "emo"*, Kathryn thought. Cam looked back at the floor.

"Great, Cam," Kathryn responded. "So technically, since you are under 18, what we speak about can be accessed by your mom. I certainly want to protect your privacy, but I will tell your mom about anything that affects your safety."

"And Mom," Kathryn continued, nodding at Abby. "To the extent that you want Cam to trust me, don't ask a bunch of questions about our sessions," Kathryn smiled.

"Ok," Abby agreed. Kathryn continued with her intake paperwork, pointing out her policies on emergencies, payments, cancelled appointments and no-shows, and explaining informed consent. Abby fidgeted in her chair. She was a tall, athletic looking woman. *She looks young and high energy*, Kathryn thought. *Kind of an LL Bean mom.*

"We're here because Camilla," Abby began, then hesitated. "I mean, sorry, wants to be on hormonal replacement therapy. We want to support him in any way possible, I mean we have been supportive this whole time, and will just do anything. But you know we are not sure that a lot of these symptoms and stuff may be depression. Or anxiety." Abby paused. "She's had a tough time with social situations all her life, she's shy. And so, we want to make sure that what is going on is transgender identity and not depression and anxiety."

"Well, there's not necessarily going to be a clear delineation," Kathryn explained. "The world is not kind to transpeople or to any person in the sexual minority, and the stress of living in a world that constantly implicitly and explicitly rejects you is going to contribute to some of this depression and anxiety."

They both nodded. Kathryn finished the part of the interview that needed a parent, then ushered the mother to the lobby so she could speak alone to Cam.

A Real Boy

Kathryn closed the door as Abby settled in the lobby and returned to her chair in front of Cam. She noticed he was tearful and as he looked up at her, his tears increased.

"I have been wanting this, like asking to go to therapy, for like over a year!" Cam began through sobs.

"I am glad you finally got here," Kathryn said quietly. "Sounds like you have had quite a lot bottled up."

"They were, they were ok when I said I was a lesbian. I was like 11 or 12, and they just kind of said, ok, whatever," Cam continued. "But slowly I started to think, it is not just that I like women romantically. It's that I actually don't feel like a girl at all and I feel like a guy."

"I just hated it when I had to do girly things, and I didn't want to act like the other girls did," Cam said. "And I didn't know trans was a thing until I was like 12 or 13, and then I thought 'oh, oh well that's, you know, that's what I am.'"

Kathryn nodded supportively as Cam went on.

"I was like really tormented about it because I just had a sense they would not be ok. So when I told them, my mom burst into tears and my dad shut down. Like never going to talk about that and pretend it isn't happening. They still deadname me. Well, except my sister. She was like you know, 'I'll call you whatever you want.'"

Kathryn smiled, and Cam continued.

"But like at my school they won't use my name and they use the dead one which is like the pinkest name ever. Even though I said not to, but they just laugh and stuff and think I'm a freak. And I go to restaurants and I feel like I pass as a boy visually, but as soon as I open my mouth, I feel like all of a sudden people are like, 'you aren't a "real" boy.'"

Cam continued crying, and Kathryn noted it seemed to be becoming more difficult for him to speak at all. His speech began sort of breaking and halting as the session came to an end.

Mismatched Memories

After two more sessions, Kathryn had made good progress with Cam in managing depression and anxiety. But Abby was somewhat hesitant to get involved in sessions. Kathryn asked her to join them for an update.

"We were really supportive for the social transition," Abby began after greeting Kathryn politely. "Dressing like a boy, that sort of thing, the haircut. It is fine."

"But the HRT," Abby continued. "I mean, well, do people ever change their minds about this kind of thing? I mean I understand now, but …"

Maybe I should meet with her alone, Kathryn thought. *I wish she wouldn't say things like that in front of this kiddo.*

"You know," Kathryn responded, "the information about this, all the statistics about this, are pretty readily available to you. I am sure you have read lots of information. So, do people's understandings of themselves evolve over time? Sure. Does that mean HRT is not appropriate? Not necessarily. This is a medical decision as well as a social decision."

"You need to consult a psychiatrist," Kathryn continued. "My letter, even if I wrote one, would not be enough. You need to be checking in with a psychiatrist. And anyway, with the distress Cam is experiencing, a psychiatrist might give you some symptomatic relief. Cam needs to be evaluated first, before I do anything. By a psychiatrist, not a primary care doctor."

"This is a lot to think about," Abby said sadly. "But I will do anything. Anything."

"It is indeed a lot to think about. HRT, talking about someone who is biologically female transitioning to male has irreversible changes," Kathryn explained. "Particularly during puberty. The voice permanently lowers and there is no reversibility around that. It completely cuts off the puberty process of a developing female body. So the repercussions of taking HRT are potentially huge. Well, not potentially huge, just huge. And the fact that you are injecting yourself with testosterone can affect your mood stability, which I always say to folks considering this, whether it is testosterone or the cocktail of drugs to transition to female. I say, you know, this can affect your emotions. This can affect depression. This can affect anxiety. It can affect anger management and aggression and all of that stuff. So, you know, we need a plan to manage that."

"You really do seem like you are willing to help Cam," Kathryn continued supportively. "What about Cam's dad?"

"Same as me," Abby responded. "We want to do the right thing and the most important thing is our child. We did decide to do the name change before school starts though, so we will solve that. That way there won't be problems at school."

"Wow," Kathryn exclaimed. "That is a great start. But it's a process, it takes a while. Some places you have to get a judge who is ok with it and you have to announce in the paper for three weeks or whatever that you are changing your name. There is court and paperwork, the newspaper thing, then back to court and the judge changing your name and declaring you with another name. Some people just don't get it all done."

"We will," Abby nodded. "If it will make things better, we will do it."

"How about if I talk to just Cam a little bit?" Kathryn asked. Abby left quietly.

"Whatever," Cam said, rolling his eyes dismissively as Abby left the room. "I have nagged at her for months and she gets all 'I'm too busy, I'm overwhelmed, this is too much' and it never happens."

"The name change, you mean?" Kathryn asked.

"Yeah," Cam continued. "And there is nothing I can do about it. I'm not even 16. I can't drive. I can't you know, sign anything. My mom has to sign off on everything. And she says she will, but she won't. She won't do it."

"You don't think she will?" Kathryn pondered. "It can be difficult for parents."

"She says that, but then she is all 'you are my little girl, I love my sweet little girl, I'm losing her and it is just too much,'" Cam said with a mocking tone. "And then I walk into the living room and she has all these baby pictures and these girly little frilly dress pictures all spread out and she is crying. And I feel more and more horrible."

"Do you feel like she supports the HRT?" Kathryn asks.

"No way," Cam responded. "And you know, if she just said like 'you can start when you're 16, or when you, you know, when you have a job or whatever,' or like just say anything. But she is just like 'we have to wait until I don't feel bad about it anymore.' Until SHE doesn't feel bad! Well, THAT is never going to happen."

This is kind of a mess, Kathryn thought. *How can I find some common ground that's respectful of the valid concerns that Mom has but is also respectful of how distressing this feels for the kid? And this mom is asking for a letter about HRT, right?*

Kathryn Chase closed the door gently behind Abby and Cam as they left the building. She sat down in her comfortable striped wingchair to think a moment about what had just occurred. *Cam deserves to have what he needs to be himself, but I don't feel right about the differences in how he and Abby describe Cam's level of support at home. And well, this is a pretty young kid and there is a part of me that worries about injecting large doses of testosterone into a vulnerable teenager.*

No Show

"Hello?" Kathryn answered as her phone rang two weeks later. "This is Kathryn Chase."

"Hello. This is Abby Murphy," Abby said cooly. "I have a charge on my bill that is for an appointment that I did not attend."

"Right," Kathryn answered. "Remember our first session? I read aloud my policy about the charge for missed appointments."

"Well that is ridiculous," Abby countered. "I should not have to pay for nothing."

"I know school gets busy. And I could provide you another copy of my initial documents if you want. Or let's make a follow up appointment that will work for you and we could talk then."

"Really though, are you going to write a letter for the HRT?" Abby asked abruptly. "Or not?"

15 Evie's Urges

Dani looked out the window, thinking as she stared at the yellow leaves of the oak tree outside of Oaklawn Solutions, Inc. She brought her attention back to the woman on the phone.

"Dani," Grace Sanders said tearfully, "I can't do this. I don't know what else to try and I am not able to keep going on like this. She can't be out of school, I can't control her. I can't keep doing this to my boys either, it just isn't fair to them."

Dani opened her mouth to empathize with Grace's frustration and to restate the plan they had developed, together, to focus on positive reinforcement for Evie instead of emphasizing what she was doing wrong. However, the words were stuck in her throat. *Maybe it's true, Evie shouldn't remain in the home with her mother and younger brothers,* Dani thought sadly. *Do I have what it takes to help Evie? I feel like I have failed her.*

Growing up in Norman, OK

Norman was a classic, nostalgic university town in the heart of Oklahoma. Just a 20-minute drive from the sprawling, urban Oklahoma City, Norman had a population of 122,000, most of whom were college students. The University of Oklahoma, "The Sooners," was the main employer of the town. Other big employers included Norman Regional Hospital, the Norman Public Schools, and Hitachi, but the culture of the University assured most everyone was a Sooner fan.

The Norman Public School system had approximately 16,000 students, 58% of whom were white and 49% were on the Free and Reduced Lunch program. The school system had a reputation for providing excellent services for students with disabilities, and had approximately 2800 children on Individualized Education Plans (IEP). Yet the state of Oklahoma had experienced tremendous cuts in education spending, and suffered dire consequences in the funding of public education. The good intentions of the school system were often challenged by the realities of limited resources, underpaid teachers, and a shortage of qualified teachers as many teachers, understandably, often left the state.

Dani Higgins, MSW, LCSW

Danielle "Dani" Higgins graduated in 2012 with her MSW from the University of Oklahoma in Norman. She was an advanced standing student, highly motivated, and she completed the program on a full-time basis. After graduation, she joined a small practice with a child psychiatrist and two other fairly recently licensed social work graduates. After completing supervision for licensure, she started her own private practice, but was able to office in the same building and continued to work with the same trusted colleagues.

Dani had been a non-traditional student, and was married with two adult sons. Her oldest, Ben, was on the Autism spectrum and recently graduated from St. Louis University with double degrees in Engineering and Math. Her youngest, Jayden, was a senior at the University of Kansas majoring in Biochemical Engineering. But it was Dani's experience as a mother of Ben that inspired her to pursue a career in social work. *Ben got beat up by the system,* Dani would tell others. *He had Asperger's before it was cool and nobody knew what it was. We went from place to place and he had all sorts of diagnoses and labels that didn't fit. And I was part of a lot of interventions that hurt him. I kept him in places that inflicted trauma with their rigid application of applied behavioral analysis. At the time, I thought I was doing what was best, but now I know more about how they used pain to punish him when he would flap his hands or repeat himself and how they made him engage with therapy for 40 hours a week—practically every waking moment! He still deals with complex PTSD from it. I swore to him that my every last breath would be used to help make the world a better place for every kid I could possibly help. So I went back to school to learn to help families. And that is why I come to my office every day. There are beautiful, wonderful kids out there that need someone to be their voice.*

Evie and Her Mom

Grace and Evie Sanders first met with Dani about three years ago when Evie was 10 years old. Evie was a beautiful little girl, with pale white skin, a sprinkle of freckles across her nose, long dark curls, and a happy smile. She was warm and friendly, immediately running up to Dani on their first session.

"Hi, I'm Evie," she had exclaimed with a wave. "I like dogs. Do you have kids? Will you be my friend?"

Her mother, Grace, had been cooler, seeming a little embarrassed at her daughter's behavior.

"She does that," Grace had said apologetically. "Never met a stranger!"

Grace was an attractive woman, small and thin, neatly groomed and well spoken. She was a single mother, also with two boys who were ages 9 and 7. She had been divorced from the children's father for two years. He spoke to the children on the phone often, but rarely visited. But he was consistent with child support and this and food stamps created their meager income.

Evie was diagnosed with an intellectual disability in second grade, a particularly late diagnosis, especially after being in early childhood programs that usually recognized developmental delays. She had met all her physical developmental milestones and no delays were noted by pediatricians. But when the school work became more challenging, Evie started refusing to complete school work and acting out at home. She was finally tested for intellectual disabilities and received a 55 as an IQ score.

The family was referred by Evie's psychiatrist, Dr. Loretta Cain, to help the family learn strategies for dealing with Evie's challenging behaviors experienced in the fifth grade. Evie had been moved to a different classroom and seemed to regress.

"In the past, Evie had some trouble with acting out, but she played with her dolls and didn't seem to have so many problems," Grace had explained. "But this year, she is hiding under the desk, crying, picking up trash and eating it, refusing to get off the floor, and that is all since she moved to the new room."

Dani helped advocate with the school to solve some of these problems by returning Evie to a self-contained classroom, and in sessions she had worked with the mother on creating behavioral plans with visual charts that were easier for Evie to understand.

"Evie's working memory and processing scores on her testing are very low," Dani had explained to Grace. "What that means to me is that it is really difficult for her to receive information, hold it there, and manipulate it in her mind. So if we say something like 'pick up your toys' she may not understand what we mean. And if we say 'put the stuffed animals in the toy box, the Legos in the bucket, and the clothes in the drawer' or whatever, she probably can't retain all of that and follow through. So let's try making a visual chart that shows her where every item belongs, so she can proceed one step at a time."

Grace always eagerly agreed to new plans and diligently tried to implement them. But by the next week's session, she had usually given up on the intervention. Evie would have been angry and ripped up a visual chart, hit or screamed when redirected, refused to comply with a request, or done something to embarrass Grace in public, and Grace would return to the session desperate and defeated.

The Urge to Bite

"Evie, I am glad to see you again!" Dani smiled at the young girl in the seat across from her. Evie had just returned home from a voluntary two-week stay at the Rosenheim Residential Treatment Center, where Grace had taken her following an episode of hitting, screaming, and throwing toys at her mother. "How long has it been, about three weeks?"

"Yeah, I think so." Evie sat on the carpeted floor, and looked down at her hands on her lap. "I missed being home with my mom and my cat. I didn't miss my brothers, they are dumb."

"Now that you have been home for a few days," Dani began, "tell me how things are going at home?" Dani made eye contact with Evie as she asked the question.

"Ok. Mom bought me pizza for dinner." Evie smiled, looking over at her mother who sat in a chair beside her. "I like having my cat sleep with me."

"Your mom mentioned that you get angry sometimes," Dani asked. "Tell me about this morning when you were getting ready to come see me. What happened before you left the house?"

"I was watching TV with my brothers and Mom was yelling at me to brush my teeth. When I got up to brush my teeth, my brothers changed the channel to some stupid show. I was mad, mad, mad."

"I wasn't yelling," Grace interjected. "But it is like this all the time, 'I need you to go to school,' 'let's get ready it's time to get in the car,' 'let's go eat dinner,' 'let's go to bed,' 'let's take a shower,' it doesn't matter. Anything you ask, if she doesn't like it, you're gonna get bit."

"OK," Dani nodded. "But let's stick with the TV and the brothers for another minute. On a scale of 0–10, Evie, how angry were you when your brothers changed the channel?"

"I was a big 9! They can't do that! I was watching TV first! They are dumb and I like the princess show and not the stupid one. I felt so mad! And Mom came in yelling at ME not them and 'BE QUIET EVIE!' 'SHUT UP!' and I …"

"And you bit me!" Grace exclaimed. She raised her arm and showed an angry red bite mark on her forearm.

"Evie," Dani nodded and looked back at her client, "can you tell me what is going on right before you need to bite? I really want to know what thoughts you have going through your mind right then, right that second."

"Mad!" Evie shouted.

"OK," Dani nodded. "How about in your body? Where do you feel this urge to bite?"

"In my tits!" Evie scowled, slapping her chest. "I feel it in my tits and it won't go away until I bite my mom."

Dani was caught off guard by this statement, though she knew how to mask her shock at the sometimes bizarre statements that came from clients. *Her tits?* Dani thought. *Is it part of her sexual development? Because she is 13 and developing? Is she having thoughts and desires and the sensations are getting confused? So she is acting out more aggressively because it helps her feel better?*

"I wonder if some of it is because she just found out her dad is getting remarried?" Grace offered. "I don't know, maybe she is mad at me somehow. Or just mad about all the charts around the house. Which she just rips up and throws on the ground, by the way." Grace looked over at Evie.

"Your dad is getting remarried?" Dani said to Evie. "How do you feel about that?"

Evie was silent and looked at the floor. She shifted her position and knocked over her soda that was resting on the coffee table and it spilled on the carpet.

"Oh no, Evie!" Grace exclaimed, jumping to her feet and dashing out of the room.

"No big deal," Dani said calmly. "I have a rug with polka dots for a reason." She opened her desk drawer and removed a roll of paper towels, handing them to Evie who began to blot up the soda.

Grace returned with wet towels from the bathroom and began to clean the spill as well.

"Time to go, Evie," Grace said firmly. "Remember our routine for today? It is Tuesday, and that is the day we have chicken for dinner and then we wash your hair and get your red clothes ready for school on Wednesday." She grabbed Evie's hand and led her to the hallway. Grace then looked back at the carpet and ran back in to blot the carpet again.

"It's really OK, Grace," Dani said. "The carpet is fine. But I guess you are right that we are out of time, so let's talk about this next time?"

A Mom on the Beach

After Grace and Evie left, Dani opened her file cabinet and took out Evie's record. She thumbed through some worksheets she had worked on with Evie last year. One was about feelings.

Evie had written in answers in large shaky handwriting about different emotions. Dani remembered how long and hard they had both worked to get through the worksheets. Under a happy face and the phrase "I feel happy when…" she wrote "smiel" meaning "smile." Under a sad face with the phrase "I feel sad when" she wrote "cry." Dani remembered trying to help her understand the difference between what other people might see on the outside versus what she feels inside, but Evie struggled to understand.

The next page was an outline of a person and titled "How Angry Feels." It pointed to different body parts with things like "My Ears Feel…," "My Belly Feels," and so on. Evie had written "bad" in most of the blanks, but Dani remembered they had some discussion with that worksheet about "bad" means she feels like jumping and hitting sometimes.

The next page was a "when you grow up" set of questions that Dani asked her and asked her to fill in. "When I grow up, I want to…" "Mom and Baby," Evie wrote. "When I grow up, I want to live…" "Beech," she wrote. "When I grow up I hope I…" "Baby and huzben."

Sweet Evie, Dani thought. *So hard for her, but she just wants to be a mom and a wife with a happy life like many other little girls. I just hope she gets that someday.*

What Now?

Dani decided to staff the case with Evie's doctor, Dr. Loretta Cain. Dr. Cain was a child psychiatrist with 20 years of experience serving children with complex mental health needs and their families, and Dani trusted her input. She had talked with her many times about Evie, but hoped some new ideas might emerge. Dr. Cain had a reputation for engaging with some of the most challenging kids and utilizing personalized and innovative treatments for young kids with reactive detachment disorder, intellectual disabilities, and Autism.

"I have been working with Evie and her family for three years," said Dani. "Three years! And she just seems to be getting worse! I was reviewing her past treatments and we have tried so many different things to modify behavior and alter this family's dynamics. I have worked with her mother on redirection, positive reinforcement, and setting clear and firm limits. We have talked about what triggers her outbursts and how to try to stop them before they start, when to ignore behaviors and when to comfort her. We have created a zillion charts to help direct Evie's behavior. They utilize these tools for about 24 hours and then as soon as a stressor hits, they are reverting to the same pattern. Mom yells and Evie responds with dysfunctional behaviors that are escalating in severity. Her mom has severe bite marks on her arms every week. I recently learned that Evie is starting to bite the teacher's aide at school!"

"I saw Evie just before she went into the Rosenheim Residential Treatment Center," said Dr. Cain. "I see from the discharge report that Evie's medications were altered, they put her back on these high doses of Risperdal and I was working to slowly titrate her off of that so we could try a smaller dose of Seroquel and see if that helped calm her more," Dr. Cain remarked with a frustrated tone. "I have an appointment with Evie and her mother next month. I will see if we can move that up a couple of weeks. We will be in a tough spot if Evie continues to have these behavior challenges at school," sighed Dr. Cain.

"In the meantime," Dani said. "I have been trying to find activities that she could participate in. I want her to socialize more and have more to do outside of the house. But it is so hard to find an activity that can handle full on Evie!"

"I bet!" Dr. Cain said with a gentle smile. "You know though, I am sure it still helps the mother to have someone listen and treat her with understanding. I know that doesn't sound like much, but sometimes as you know, moms start to feel pretty alone out there."

"Thank you," said Dani. "I really appreciate your support. I guess I will keep trying to help Grace handle these behaviors somehow. But I just can't help thinking that I am missing something in my treatment planning with Evie."

Worrisome New Behavior

The morning of Dani's next appointment with Evie was an unusually warm fall day. She remembered to tune into the weather later in the day, as there was a chance of severe storms around the time Evie and Grace were due for their session. Dani had just opened up the weather app when the phone rang.

"Hello?" Dani said.

"Dani, I am so glad I caught you!" cried Grace. "I really need to talk with you before you meet with Evie."

"What's going on, Grace?" Dani could hear the urgency in Grace's voice.

"The school just called and demanded I come pick up Evie. They wouldn't tell me what was wrong over the phone. When I got there, they took me right into the principal's office and, oh God." She sighed. Grace swallowed hard. "They told me that when Evie was working at the computer center during class she became angry with another student. This other student, he wanted to use the computer so he was asking Evie to move. She, I can't believe she did this at school, but remember that thing I told you she was doing a couple months ago at home? To get her brothers away from her? She did that at school! The school said she can't be there if she is going to do that. It's just too awful. What am I going to do if she gets kicked out of school?"

Dani definitely remembered. Several sessions ago, Grace had mentioned this behavior to her at the end of their session. When Evie had been fighting with her brothers and wanted them to get away from her, she would put her hands down her pants, rub her hands all over her genitalia and then flick whatever she came up with on her fingers at her brothers. *To get people to go away,* Dani had thought, *that would be incredibly effective.*

"Oh, Grace, I am sorry to hear that. But let's talk about it with Evie at 3 during our session," Dani said gently. *We were both hoping Evie would not do this as school,* Dani thought. *They can't deal with that at school. We talked about telling her to stop but trying not to shame her or act horrified, but just be firm. But there is no teacher, no classroom that can deal with kids who are feeling the need to bite in their tits and are wiping their genitalia and flicking it around. And she can't keep doing that around her brothers, either. We have to get her to stop it somehow.*

"Dani," Grace said tearfully, "I can't do this. I don't know what else to try and I am not able to keep going on like this. She can't be out of school, I can't control her. I can't keep doing this to my boys either, it just isn't fair to them."

Dani opened her mouth to empathize with Grace's frustration and to restate the plan they had developed, together, to focus on positive reinforcement for Evie instead of emphasizing what she was doing wrong. However, the words were stuck in her throat. *Maybe it's true, Evie shouldn't remain in the home with her mother and younger brothers,* Dani thought sadly. *Do I have what it takes to help Evie? I feel like I have failed her. Are we really at the end of the road on outpatient services?*

16 You're Doing This Wrong

"Things aren't looking good for you," Ann whispered as she glanced out of the elevator to make sure no one could hear her. An insistent ding filled the small space as the elevator door attempted to close, repeatedly tapping Ashley's hand every few seconds. Ann, the office manager, seemed flustered as she leaned in and continued, "they're interviewing everyone about how you handled the situation with Adam."

Ashley noticed that her cheeks were beet-red as she caught a glimpse of her reflection in the elevator mirror while the door closed, ending her informal meeting with Ann. *I'm just trying to do what is best for our clients,* Ashley thought as she walked back to her office. *What they are asking me to do will hurt Adam and he'll probably end up back in the hospital … or worse. How can I promote change in this agency without losing my job?*

A Busy Year

2017 was an eventful year for Ashley Miller. She started a new job as clinical director with Youth Treatment Innovations (YTI), an Austin-based partial hospitalization program (PHP) that hired her to spearhead their expansion in San Antonio. Ashley had been a licensed clinical social worker for several years leading up to this new opportunity, but she had no supervisory or administrative experience prior to accepting the position at YTI. She didn't want to completely give up the direct practice aspect of her work, so she also launched a small private practice where she saw clients in the evenings. In the midst of all these changes, she also planned a wedding and married her long-time boyfriend.

These new roles in Ashley's life mirrored an internal sense of personal growth. She emanated professionalism and confidence, yet the shoulder tattoos that often peeked out from under her shirt sleeves were reminders of her free spirit and adventurous early-adulthood. A self-described millennial in her early 30s, Ashley was increasingly focused on her career and ready to settle down. During graduate school she worked as a bartender between practicum at the VA and classes at the University of Texas at Austin. She spent her first few post-MSW years working in an HIV clinic in Austin, but her desire to pursue clinical licensure led her to apply for a clinical social work position at an outpatient mental health clinic in San Antonio.

The Holiday Party

The administrative opportunity at YTI wasn't something Ashley had been actively seeking out, and she often told people that the job found *her*. She first met Dr. Michael Evans at a holiday party in late 2016. As the host introduced Ashley to Dr. Evans, she recognized the woman he had been talking to as Dr. Celia Graham—a well-known medical director for the psychiatric unit at Methodist Texan Hospital in San Antonio. She came to learn that Dr. Evans had been a practicing psychiatrist in the Austin area for decades and that he had founded YTI—one of the first PHPs in the region.

As Ashley shared about her experience as a Licensed Clinical Social Worker (LCSW), Dr. Evans interrupted her, "I've been trying to convince Dr. Graham here to join me in starting a YTI branch in San Antonio!" He smiled at Ashley and then back at Dr. Graham. "It seems that fate has brought us together!"

Having experienced many networking opportunities that amounted to nothing more than a fun conversation, Ashley was pleasantly surprised by Dr. Evan's frequent emails and phone calls in the months following the holiday party. At first, he offered her a role as the lead therapist at the San Antonio YTI expansion, but months of unsuccessful efforts to recruit a clinical director culminated in him offering the position to Ashley. Informal meetings and communications gradually transitioned to more formal interviews, and by the summer of 2017 Ashley gave notice to her employer so she could begin her work as the clinical director of YTI San Antonio.

Youth Treatment Innovations

YTI was one of the most successful PHPs in the Austin-Round Rock metropolitan area. The Austin office was the original YTI location and had been very successful since its launch in 2008. Their census usually held steady at around 80 clients, half male and half female. They admitted youth between the ages of 4 and 18 who were often placed in YTI after being discharged from intensive inpatient psychiatric treatment. Although YTI clients were considered high needs, they could not pose an immediate risk to themselves or others to be considered for the program.

Most of the administrative staff at the Austin office had been with the YTI since the beginning. Although Dr. Evans was the CEO and founder of the organization, he could easily be mistaken for a therapist, given his hands-on approach to running the agency. He ate lunch in the client cafeteria and was frequently seen on the units and in the classrooms. The kids came to know him as Dr. Mike, and he clearly found enjoyment in being closely connected to the important work being done at YTI. Although he was the visionary who launched the program, it was no secret that Dr. Evans despised the financial, regulatory, and bureaucratic aspects of running a large PHP. For these things, he leaned heavily on the executive director, Madison Jones.

A single mother in her late 30s, Madison had started her career at YTI as a Registered Nurse and was promoted to executive director in 2013. She had no training as a counselor or administrator, but knew the inner workings of YTI better than anyone. She was directly involved in everything from financial planning to curriculum selection. She was the driving force behind the expansion of YTI outside of Austin and had personally launched satellite programs in Georgetown and San Marcos. Madison was also very involved in the San Antonio expansion effort.

The CFO, Tiffany Churchill, was another long-time employee who had been promoted from within the agency. A Licensed Professional Counselor (LPC), Tiffany started her career as a therapist in the program before she was promoted to the role of CFO. She was a quick study and her lack of formal financial training did not keep her from successfully managing YTI's growing financial complexity.

As YTI's regional footprint increased, the Austin office maintained tight control of nearly all operations. Referrals and contacts were all processed by the admissions department in Austin, regardless of the requested placement site. Madison and Tiffany had office space in each of the satellite locations and they both made a point of dropping in at each location frequently. The clinical directors at each site reported directly to Madison and were expected to attend semi-monthly administrative meetings in Austin.

From the Ground Up

During her first few months at YTI, Ashley commuted from San Antonio to Austin several times per week to observe operations at the YTI-Austin program and prepare for her new administrative duties. When she wasn't in Austin, her days were filled with zoning meetings, staff interviews, and tours of prospective locations for the San Antonio PHP.

By mid-summer, Dr. Evans signed a lease for a two-story medical complex northwest of downtown San Antonio. Although it was a great location with convenient access from the 410 Loop, it had previously housed several doctors' offices and a dental practice and the space needed extensive renovations to comply with state regulations and licensing for PHPs. While Dr. Evans and administrative staff in Austin managed most of the renovations and contracting, it was left to Ashley to make thousands of decisions, large and small, as they worked feverishly to meet a projected Fall 2017 launch of YTI-San Antonio.

Most of the initial renovations focused on the first floor of the building, where classrooms, groups rooms, a padded "calm room," a cafeteria, and therapist offices were quickly constructed. The second floor received less priority since it was to be used for administrative offices. The weeks flew by as Ashley spent her days assembling furniture, hanging pictures, and ordering supplies. Slowly, but surely, the space began to look like a proper PHP.

Early on, Ashley decided that she would like her office to be on the first floor instead of with the rest of the administrative staff on the second floor. *I want to have as much contact with our clients and my staff as possible.* Ashley selected an office right inside the main entrance to the facility, across from the elevator to the administrative offices. *This way I can be accessible to the staff and clients in the program and I can easily pop upstairs whenever I'm needed.*

Bathroom Signs

As the renovation of client bathrooms neared completion, Ashley spent a morning buying toilet paper and soap dispensers, paper towel mounts, and bathroom signs at a local hardware store. YTI bathroom policies for clients were very specific. The bathrooms were to be locked at all times and clients could only use them when accompanied by a staff member who would unlock the restroom and wait outside while it was in use. Although it was assumed that the two renovated restrooms would be designated by gender, it occurred to Ashley that they would almost certainly admit transgender clients and that it might be best to use gender neutral signs. By that same evening, the bathroom fixtures had been installed.

A few days passed before Madison visited the facility to survey the construction progress. "We need to talk," Madison said, inviting herself into Ashley's office, "can you please explain why you installed gender neutral bathroom signs?"

Although Ashley had intuited that the reason for Madison's unplanned meeting would not be pleasant, she was unprepared to answer the question. A few awkward moments passed before she responded, "I guess I was thinking that we should have facilities that are welcoming to our clients regardless of their gender identity."

"We can't have shared gender bathrooms for safety reasons," Madison's tone was firm and decisive.

"I guess I don't understand how this is a safety problem," Ashley felt her face flush as she continued, "The doors will always be locked and kids only use the restroom one at a time. They are always accompanied by a staff member." Madison's response was firm and clearly communicated that the discussion was over, "Listen, I've been running PHPs for years and I know all too well how dangerous it can be when we don't have strict bathroom policies. These kids will go in there and do all sorts of things that are against the rules." Ashley still didn't follow exactly how the gender neutral bathrooms would be any different from binary bathrooms, but she resisted the urge to argue with Madison. "You need to take the signs down and return them today and I'll order appropriate signs to be delivered later this week," Madison said as she stood and left Ashley's office.

As she drove to the hardware store to return the signs, Ashley couldn't shake the feeling that she was being disciplined. *I don't understand why they would hire me to be a clinical director and to set up this whole program if they are going to micromanage every little thing. More importantly, what will we do when a transgender client is admitted? I know the State of Texas has been pretty hostile to gender and sexual minorities, but surely YTI isn't transphobic...*

Maiden Voyage

The weeks leading up to the official launch of YTI-San Antonio were a blur. Ashley was mostly focused on training new clinicians and support staff, but she also had a bottomless to-do list of last-minute preparations before the first clients were admitted. Client transportation plans had to be finalized and San Antonio Independent School District (SAISD) teachers needed training and orientation. A special education teacher was assigned to the facility and last-minute preparations were being made to ensure that the facility followed state IEP regulations.

The chaotic schedule was accentuated by continued renovation projects throughout the facility. A stack of "calm room" padding rolls cluttered the hallway right outside of Ashley's office and frequent bangs and thuds rattled the walls as workers continued to remodel the administrative offices on the second floor.

In the flurry of activity, Ashley periodically took a moment to check the Electronic Medical Record system (EMR) to monitor her expected census for YTI-San Antonio's maiden voyage. She was a little uncomfortable with the admission process and thought it weird that referrals had to speak with the Austin intake department by phone to be accepted into the program. Still, it was reassuring to see the client list grow.

In the week leading up to the start of services, Ashley dropped all her other projects to focus on scheduling intake interviews and assessments with clients who had been accepted into the program by YTI-Austin. Each client was to be assigned to a primary therapist. Ashley had already hired three therapists and several rehab specialists, so she attempted to evenly distribute the initial wave of referrals amongst the staff.

The first few weeks of programing at YTI-San Antonio were as busy as Ashley had imagined. Most of her time was spent coordinating the logistics of the program. It took hours to streamline the transportation route for a staff member to pick up clients as efficiently as possible in the agency van. Although YTI-San Antonio had a small kitchen in the cafeteria, Ashley had arranged for SAISD to provide breakfast and lunch each day. She spent the first hour of her day trying to get an accurate head count so she could order the proper amount of meals and she often had to pick them up herself from a nearby elementary school.

Depending on their age, clients would start their day in rehab or educational groups. Older clients spent the morning in therapeutic groups while the younger clients attended school. The groups would switch after lunch. The goal was to split the clients by age and gender into cohorts: a young boys' group, an older boys' group, a young girls' group, and an older girls' group. Per YTI policy, each cohort was capped at eight clients. Ashley soon came to dread the morning portion of the program as most behavioral outbursts tended to happen during the educational portion of the program with the younger clients. Ashley and her staff had been trained in verbal de-escalation and therapeutic restraints, but she did not envision the need to use the latter very frequently.

The therapeutic groups were mostly led by rehab specialists, and therapists would pull clients out for individual sessions throughout the week. Ashley made it a top priority to maintain a high standard of clinical practice in the agency and she insisted on capping clinician caseloads at ten. This goal quickly clashed with the growing census, and Ashley began to take a small caseload of her own to keep up with demand. Challenges of the cohort model were apparent when the age and gender of referrals didn't neatly line up with program availability.

As the first few weeks passed, Ashley felt an increased comfort in her new role as clinical director. *I really wish I had waited to launch my private practice. I'm exhausted! But it is gratifying to make such a meaningful difference in the lives of so many clients and I'm actually pretty good at this director stuff.*

You're Doing this Wrong

Tiffany and Madison made frequent trips to the new YTI-San Antonio office and Ashley could feel the tension in the building rise whenever they showed up unannounced, often together. During one of their visits, Tiffany wandered onto the client units to observe the program. "You're doing this wrong—didn't anyone train you on how to lead a group?" Tiffany said to Joshua, one of the more inexperienced rehab specialists. She then pulled up a chair and proceeded to take over the remaining 25 minutes of group time.

"I know that I still have lots to learn, but I don't understand why she embarrassed me like that in front of the kids," Joshua told Ashely later that day.

"I'm so sorry that happened," Ashley said empathetically, "she used to be a therapist in Austin, so I'm sure she was just trying to help." Despite her effort to comfort Joshua, Ashley was bothered by the incident that was increasingly common when Tiffany and Madison were in the building. *Surely things will improve as the program gets going. It must be hard for them to oversee so many different sites, but I wish they would bring concerns about staff to my attention and let me handle it.*

Elizabeth is Adam

Several months into the program, Ashley felt as though things had finally settled down. The census was stable and staff appeared to be adjusting to their roles in the agency. Ashely had made it a habit of keeping an eye on admission referrals from Austin on a daily basis. The EMR system allowed her to keep track of the wait list and she could also monitor the volume of referrals. In particular, Ashley closely monitored referrals that were "red flagged," which was an informal way of coding clients who were being admitted after discharge from an inpatient psychiatric facility. Ashley felt strongly that red flagged admissions needed to be expedited whenever possible.

For several weeks Ashley had seen Elizabeth Redfield's name in the admission list, and she was happy to see that the Redfield family had actually shown up for their intake assessment the previous evening and that she had been formally admitted into the program. Elizabeth had missed three previous intake appointments at YTI-San Antonio. Although Ashley did not know the specific reasons for the missed appointments with Elizabeth, she had grown accustomed to this pattern with "red flagged" referrals since these clients were often readmitted to hospitals for regressions related to self-harm and suicide.

Later that morning, Ashley ran into rehab specialist Antonio in the hallway and asked him how Elizabeth was adjusting to the program. "Yeah, about that ... you know you put a girl in my boy's group, right?"

"Oh," Ashley stalled as she processed Antonio's statement and eventually responded, "is it going to be a problem for you or the group?"

"I'm cool with it," Antonio shrugged his shoulders and continued, "can she go boxing with the rest of us this Friday?"

"Of course!" Ashley answered as Antonio walked back to the unit.

I wonder how we will address the bathroom situation, Ashley thought as she walked to Joshua's office to talk about Elizabeth's admission. In the month since the program had started, Joshua had already been promoted to be the rehab specialist manager.

"Yeah, so it turns out that Elizabeth is Adam," Joshua correctly guessed the reason for Ashley's visit. "I figured you would want to place him in the older boy's group since that is his gender identity, so I put him with Antonio."

"Did you ask him about his gender identity?" Ashley asked cautiously.

"Well, not really. It sort of just came up. When Mom dropped him off this morning I asked him what his name was and he hesitated before saying Elizabeth. Then his mom interrupted him and said that 'her name is Elizabeth, but she prefers to go by Adam and she prefers male pronouns'."

I know that Adam had been inpatient for a suicide attempt prior to his referral to us, I sure hope we are able to support him and help him get better, Ashley thought as she validated Joshua's decision. "You did exactly what I would have told you to do. Thanks."

The last thing Ashley wanted to do was to single Adam out or make him feel uncomfortable in any way, so she decided to wait and meet him after group that afternoon. The end of the day routine at YTI-San Antonio was chaotic as dozens of kids piled into the agency vans while others were greeted by their parents and guardians in the lobby.

It wasn't hard to pick Adam out in the crowd. An overweight kid walked into the lobby with short hair and large breasts that appeared to have been tightly bound. "You must be Adam," Ashley introduced herself with a smile, "how was your first day?"

Adam smiled and briefly made eye contact, "It was fine."

"Wonderful! I'm looking forward to seeing you again tomorrow! Please come to my office if you need anything at all." Ashley hoped that her staff and the other clients had been kind to Adam.

After the chaos had subsided, Ashley returned to her office. She sat for several moments in her office thinking about how she might best prepare her staff to work with Adam before noticing an email from Katie, the intake coordinator in Austin:

To: Ashley Miller
From: Katie Smith
Subject: Group Policy

I was just informed that you admitted Elizabeth Redfield to one of the male groups today. I am not sure what justification or assessment you used to make this decision, but you must keep in mind that administrative staff needs to be informed before you make any determination like this one. Our policy has always been to keep clients in groups according to their anatomical gender.

As you know, I have to keep a very close eye on our census and we might have to deny a male applicant if you leave this girl in the boy's group. Until you hear otherwise, it is best to transfer Elizabeth to a group for her birth gender.

Please consider this email an official admonition against making this type of impulsive decision moving forward. I will be staffing this situation with Dr. Evans, Dr. Graham, and Ms. Churchill.

Katie Jones
Intake Coordinator
Youth Treatment Innovations
Austin, Texas

Ashley was shocked as she stared at her monitor for several moments in disbelief. *I would have noticed such a transphobic policy if it were actually in our manual,* Ashley thought and she regained her composure. *I know that families have always complained about how rude Katie is on the phone. Maybe she's just being difficult. And we have five open slots for boys in our program right now. There is no current risk of a male client being denied.* Ashley's thoughts shifted to Adam. *How will he react if we move him to the girls' group? This kid has been through so much and is still recovering from a serious suicidal episode! How could we do this to him?!* Ashley composed and deleted several responses to Katie's email before she finally decided to sleep on it instead of responding in anger.

The following morning, Ashley was no less upset than when she'd first read the email. *The census argument is ridiculous! There is no way I'm going to alienate Adam. I'm just going to wait and cross this bridge if our census improves and I need to waitlist a male admit.* Ashley made the decision to keep Adam in the boys' group for the time being. Several days passed and Ashley didn't hear from anyone at YTI-Austin, so her attention shifted back to the daily challenges of running the program. Adam remained in his group and Antonio reported that he was doing well.

Unannounced Visit

Later that week, Madison and Tiffany arrived at YTI-San Antonio for an unannounced visit. They bypassed Ashley's office as they entered the building and went directly upstairs to the administrative offices. *That's strange. They almost always check in with me first. Surely this isn't about the situation with Adam?*

About an hour passed as Ashley sat in her office ruminating about the unannounced visit. She heard the elevator ding in the hallway and looked out of her door hoping to see Madison and Tiffany. Instead she saw Ann, the office manager, who was gesturing for her to come over.

"Things aren't looking good for you," Ann whispered as she glanced out of the elevator to make sure no one could hear her. An insistent ding filled the small space as the elevator door attempted to close, tapping Ashley's hand every few seconds. Ann seemed flustered as she leaned in and continued, "they're interviewing everyone about how you handled the situation with Adam."

Ashley noticed that her cheeks were beet-red as she caught a glimpse of her reflection in the elevator mirror while the door closed, ending her informal meeting with Ann. *I'm just trying to do what is best for our clients*, Ashley thought as she walked back to her office. *What they are asking me to do will hurt Adam and he'll probably end up back in the hospital … or worse. How can I promote change in this agency without losing my job?*

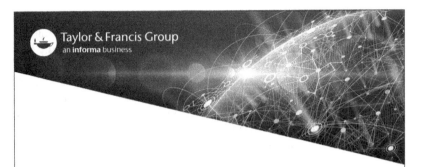